HISTORY OF THE
GREAT WESTERN
RAILWAY

HISTORY OF THE
GREAT WESTERN
RAILWAY

First published in the UK in 2014

© Demand Media Limited 2014

www.demand-media.co.uk

Printed and bound in Europe

ISBN 978-1-910270-18-9

The views in this book are those of the author but they are general views only and readers are urged to consult the relevant and qualified specialist for individual advice in particular situations. Demand Media Limited hereby exclude all liability to the extent permitted by law of any errors or omissions in this book and for any loss, damage or expense (whether direct or indirect) suffered by a third party relying on any information contained in this book.

All our best endeavours have been made to secure copyright clearance for every photograph used but in the event of any copyright owner being overlooked please address correspondence to Demand Media Limited, Waterside Chambers, Bridge Barn Lane, Woking, Surrey, GU21 6NL

Contents

4 Introduction

6 The Early Years

12 Building the Railway

22 Travelling West

34 The First Train Services

42 The Broad Gauge Locomotives

62 Expansion and Acquisition

72 Engineering Excellence: The Works

78 Engineering Excellence: The Standard Gauge Locomotives

102 Traffic and Revenue

112 The Railways Act and Grouping

116 The Great Western Branch Line

120 Nationalisation and Beyond

124 The Preservation Scene

Introduction

If you're old enough to remember the steam era of the Great Western and the Western Region then you will have some sense of what gave the railway and its locomotives such a magical appeal. Difficult to define, but a mix ranging from the sight, sound and smell of green engines adorned with copper capped chimneys and brass safety valves to summer journeys redolent of gloriously remembered holidays on the beaches and moors of Devon and Cornwall.

For enthusiasts there are countless illustrated books with detailed analyses that try to distil the enduring appeal of the Great Western Railway. These books tend to concentrate on the era after George Jackson Churchward, the engineer who defined the look and feel of the Great Western from the start of the twentieth century through to the end of steam in the 1960s. Typically these histories split the Great Western into two distinct periods: the broad gauge era and the standard gauge era with the broad gauge and early years of the company generally portrayed in much less detail.

In this book we attempt to address that deficit by detailing the early years of the company and the lives of the men who influenced its early development, reviewing both in the wider context of the way Victorian society was developing.

Some men stand out like giants in the company's early history. Brunel clearly, the man with the vision and magnetism to persuade the company's first directors to adopt the broad gauge and the circuitous but level route from London to Bristol. He is rightly remembered as one of Britain's greatest engineers, his enduring legacy the mainline route from London to Bristol,

Box Tunnel and the Royal Albert Bridge at Saltash, Cornwall. But towering alongside Brunel is the company's first Locomotive Superintendent, Daniel Gooch.

Gooch, a practical down-to-earth engineer was on hand to prevent disaster from some of Brunel's more fanciful excesses such as his first locomotive designs for the railway and the debacle over the South Devon Atmospheric Railway. Brunel is lazily credited with setting up Swindon Works but in reality the location, building and subsequent development of the Works was almost entirely the work of Gooch. From his exceptionally competent management of the Great Western's engineering requirements he went on to become the company's Chairman, rescuing it from near bankruptcy in the process. And outside the world of the Great Western Gooch became a Member of Parliament and masterminded the laying of the first trans-Atlantic telegraph cable, for which service he was created a baronet. Truly a superman.

Gooch's successor as Locomotive Superintendent was Joseph Armstrong, an engineer somewhat ignored by history. This book attempts to correct that and provides detail of his locomotives, some of which remained the basis for the design of work-horse engines through to the 1920s and 30s. A staunch Methodist, Armstrong had a strong sense of fairness and won the loyalty of the Swindon workforce, over 2,000 of whom crowded into Swindon's St Mark's churchyard for his funeral service.

Engineers have tended to define the image of the Great Western, none more so than George Jackson Churchward. With an emphasis on standardisation and a desire to incorporate the best available engineering techniques he established a set of precepts echoed in the designs of his successors Collett and Hawksworth. It's the stamp of Churchward that did so much to establish the image of the Great Western. Summer Saturdays with a Castle class loco hauling a train of chocolate and cream coaches, the journey ending on a bucolic branch line, the coaches fussily shepherded by a small pannier tank or 0-4-2 tank engine. Now, sadly, just a nostalgic memory, "Gone with Regret" to stretch the mnemonic reference.

Except it hasn't. The last chapter in this book, The Preservation Scene, shows how it is still possible to enjoy the sight sound and smell of a journey on a Great Western branch line and even experience the thrill of riding behind a Great Western express engine on a mainline steam special.

The Early Years

Incorporating the Great Western Railway

With a history dating back to the 13th Century, Bristol had become one of Britain's most important ports by the 17th and 18th Centuries, an important link in the slave trade and the largest importer of tobacco from America.

Gradual silting of the River Avon and an increase in the size of ships saw Bristol losing its primacy to Liverpool, a port with bigger and deeper docks and a convenient rail connection, the Liverpool and Manchester Railway, to the factories of Manchester and north-west England.

Conscious of plans to link London to Birmingham and Liverpool by rail and eager to retain Bristol's status as England's second port, the City's merchants saw the construction of their own railway line between Bristol and London as the solution.

In the autumn of 1832 they set up the Bristol Railway Committee and working in co-operation with London business interests the Great Western Railway was founded at a public meeting called by the Committee and held in Bristol in January 1833.

The merchants had high ambitions for their line and wanted it built to engineering standards that would out-perform the railway lines being built in the north-west and the Midlands and at the 1833 Committee meeting they confirmed the appointment as their chief engineer a man with the vision to match their ambition, the legendary Isambard Kingdom Brunel.

Though only 27, Brunel had

established his visionary engineering credentials with his radical design for the Clifton Suspension Bridge, construction of which had started in 1831. This was Brunel's first major commission, awarded to him along with a prize of 100 guineas for winning the competition for the best design to bridge the Clifton Gorge. Including Brunel, designs were submitted from a total of 22 competitors.

The Committee's first task for Brunel was a survey of the railway's route between London and Bristol. With the help of friends and colleagues, including his solicitor Jeremiah Osborne, Brunel completed the survey in just three months, ready for submission to Parliament for approval of the line's construction.

The first Great Western Railway bill encountered predictable strong opposition from landowners, notably from Eton College who contended that building the line could encourage the schoolboys to "seek the doubtful dissipations of London town".

After revision of the proposed route and inclusion in the Bill of clauses insisted upon by Eton College, Parliamentary approval was finally obtained and the Great Western Railway Act was passed on the 31st August 1835.

Above: Coat of Arms of the Great Western Railway incorporating the shields of the cities of London and Bristol

Brunel's vision

Eager for early completion of the railway the directors had already sanctioned the initial construction and planning of the route, including approval for Brunel to begin design of important structures such as the Maidenhead Bridge and the Wharncliffe Viaduct.

On the 15th September 1835, barely

two weeks after the passing of the Act, Brunel wrote to the directors of the Great Western Railway detailing both his innovative plans for constructing the new railway and his broader vision of what the Great Western could be, a company linking London and New York via Bristol. He was determined, too, that in terms of engineering excellence, speed and comfort the Great Western's railway would surpass any of the rival lines then being built in the North and the Midlands.

Today we'd describe Brunel as an entrepreneur but at a distance of almost two centuries it is perhaps hard to appreciate the sheer magnetism and charisma of the man: a man able to secure acceptance by the Board of his two very radical decisions regarding the railway's construction and also see the setting up of the Great Western Steamship Company, responsible for the *SS Great Western's* maiden voyage in 1838 and the launch of the *SS Great Britain* in 1843. But maybe not that hard to appreciate: when the BBC broadcast *100 Greatest Britons* in 2002, Isambard Kingdom Brunel, sponsored by Jeremy Clarkson, was voted second in a poll of viewers.

And those two construction decisions, fundamental to Brunel's vision of the railway and for which he won Board approval? First, he wanted to build the line from London to Swindon through the Marlborough Downs – a route with few major towns – and second, he advocated that the track should be broad gauge.

The universal adoption of standard gauge by the early railway companies happened almost by accident. The first railways, in the late 18th and early 19th centuries, were colliery lines and the gap between the rails was the minimum that could comfortably accommodate two horses pulling the coal wagons or chaldrons. As colliery mileage extended it was eventually necessary to standardise that two horse width, established initially for rough-and-ready practical reasons, as a gauge of 4'8½.

Unfettered by a colliery heritage Brunel reasoned that a broader gauge would allow larger wheels, a more stable ride and the potential for bigger, faster locomotives. Conscious, too, that steam locomotives, particularly the rudimentary ones of the 1830s, struggled on the slightest gradient, he surveyed a route towards Oxford and eventually Swindon that had virtually no gradients. Later travellers on the GWR sometimes referred disparagingly to this route as "Great Way Round" though contemporary commentators called it more charitably "Brunel's billiard table".

An error of judgement

As it turned out Brunel's judgements were broadly correct and by the mid-1840s trains on the GWR were both 25% faster and 30% heavier than rival trains on the London & Birmingham, Grand Junction and South Western railways.

But with hindsight it is clear that Brunel was guilty of a major misjudgement, not of engineering nor of railway operations, but of human nature. In 1835 railway mileage in Great Britain, built or already authorised, greatly exceeded the initial mileage proposed by the Great Western. Brunel seems to have been arrogantly confident that once his railway was running its all-round superiority would be so obvious that everyone else would be ready to change.

Wrong. That was a complete underestimate of English tenacity which, when faced with severe opposition, promptly digs in, ready to withstand a siege. And, of course the rapid spread of the 4'8½" gauge, particularly during

Opposite: *A wax sculpture of Brunel at the Swindon Steam Railway Museum*

Above: *SS Gt Britain. The world's largest ship afloat when launched in 1843*

the first wave of railway mania in the 1840s, meant that in a very short time it was Brunel himself who was completely encompassed by this so called narrow gauge.

The Royal Commission on Railway Gauges

With the extension of the broad gauge to railways connecting to and associated with the Great Western, such as the Bristol & Exeter Railway and the South Devon Railway, the situation, nationwide, looked like becoming such a muddle that Parliament set up a Royal Commission on Railway Gauges in July 1845.

Robust submissions to the Commission, particularly by Daniel Gooch, appointed by Brunel as the Great Western's Superintendent of Locomotives in 1837, clearly demonstrated the superiority of the broad gauge. Submissions from the "narrow gauge" camp, presented by such eminent engineers as George Stephenson and Joseph Locke, acknowledged the benefits of broad gauge but argued in favour of the "narrow" gauge on the grounds of uniformity, greater track mileage and the inconvenience of changing from one gauge to another at junctions.

Largely on the basis of the "narrow" gauge's total route-mileage the Commission was inclined to recommend the elimination of the broad gauge. But first the Board of Trade and then Parliament watered down the report so much that not only was the original extent of the broad gauge left intact

but by 1859 substantial extensions to Plymouth, Swansea, Haverfordwest, Weymouth, Truro and Penzance had been built.

Above:
Complicated crossing on mixed gauge track

Building the Railway

Brunel's plan

Brunel's survey proposed a route from London to Bristol that ran north of the Marlborough Downs by way of Reading and Bath. This apparently round-about route was chosen because it offered minimum gradients and would also make it easier to build subsequent extensions to Oxford, Gloucester and South Wales.

West of Reading Brunel planned a route for the railway that followed the course of the Thames through the valley of the Chilterns. For a distance of 77 miles the track would rise gradually as it proceeded west to Swindon, never exceeding a gentle rise of 8 ft per mile, while the descent to Bristol was restricted to two slightly steeper gradients of 1 in 100. One of these gradients passed through the Box Tunnel which, at a length of almost two miles was one of the line's most challenging civil engineering feats.

Brunel's survey provided for a cost of £2.8m to build the line from London to Bristol but, inevitably, unanticipated engineering problems and cost over-runs saw the final cost escalate to £6.5m.

Construction begins

Preliminary building and planning work had started before the granting of the Great Western Railway Act in 1835 but in 1836 official construction started at two separate locations: from Bristol towards Bath and from London towards Reading with a progressive reduction in the gap between Reading and Bath.

The first section of the line, 22.5 miles

Above: *Vulcan, delivered to the Great Western in November 1837 and identical to Aoelus*

from a temporary station in London to Maidenhead Bridge Station opened to traffic on the 4th June 1838. The first train was hauled by *Aoelus*, a 2-2-2 tender engine built to Brunel's specification by Charles Tayleur & Co. at their Vulcan Foundry in Newton Le Willows.

Subsequent sections of the railway were completed and opened in piece meal stages, working from both the western and eastern extremities of the line. By December 1840 the line from London had reached a temporary terminus, Wootton Bassett Road, just west of Swindon and 80 miles from Paddington.

At the railway's western end the 11.5 mile section from Bristol to Bath was completed in August 1840 so that once the section west of Wootton Bassett to Chippenham was finished at the end of May 1841 the only thing preventing direct travel from London to Bristol was the completion of Box Tunnel, one of the line's most significant engineering challenges. The tunnel opened, without any ceremony, on 30th June 1841, heralding the start of direct railway services from London to Bristol.

Engineering Challenges

Box Tunnel was not the only major civil engineering project required to preserve Brunel's near gradient free "billiard table" route from London to Bristol. Major earthworks included the Sonning cutting while the section from London to Swindon included both the Wharncliff Viaduct and the Maidstone Bridge.

Sonning cutting was dug through high ground to the east of Reading close to the village of Sonning. The original survey planned a route north of Sonning Hill which would have obviated the need for major earthworks but objections from local landowners necessitated a cutting 60 feet deep and over a mile long closely bypassing the village of Sonning. Built at the same time as the famous Tring cutting on the London and Birmingham Railway, Sonning was shorter but deeper, its depth approaching the point that would normally have required a tunnel to be bored. Without any mechanical aids the cutting had to literally be dug out by hand, the spoil removed by wheelbarrows and horse carts and construction over the two years 1836 to 1837 required over 6,000 navvies and 450 horses. Inevitably there were a number of fatalities.

From London, the first major obstacle was crossing the Brent Valley between Hanwell and Southall, Ealing. This was resolved by the Wharnecliffe Viaduct, a brick built viaduct 886 feet long consisting of 8 semi-elliptical arches 60 feet above the valley floor. The viaduct, built in 1836-7, was commissioned at a cost of £40,000 from the contracting partnership of Thomas Grissel and Samuel Morton Peto, the latter a name famous for Victorian railway building and promotion, both in Britain and overseas.

Wharnecliffe Viaduct was the first major civil engineering project contracted out by the Great Western Railway and though it's easy to imagine a versatile engineer such as Brunel taking responsibility for all aspects of the line's construction he relied heavily on a number of other engineers, such as George Thomas Clark on the civil engineering side and Daniel Gooch, appointed by Brunel as Superintendent of Locomotives in 1837.

An interesting man, an engineer as well as being a trained surgeon, Clark's construction responsibilities included bridges over the Thames at Upper Basildon and Moulsford and involvement in building Paddington station.

On the route from London the next major challenge was crossing the Thames at Maidenhead. The bridge here, Maidenhead Bridge, was entirely Brunel's work and he had begun its design even before the railway had got its Parliamentary assent.

Subsequently immortalised in J M W Turner's famous painting *Rain, Steam and Speed*, Maidenhead Bridge carries the railway across the Thames on two flattened brick arches which at the time of building were the widest and flattest in the world, each span measuring 128 ft. The inspiration for the picture happened during a violent rainstorm when, to the surprise of his fellow passengers, Turner stuck his head out of the carriage window to mentally capture the scene before collapsing, soaking wet, back into the compartment. This event, originally attributed to Turner's champion, art critic John Ruskin, is now regarded as an apocryphal myth. But it's still a good story.

Extending the network

Brunel correctly anticipated that building the Great Western Railway would attract the interest of other railway promoters eager to link up with the route from London to Bristol.

Though promoted independently most had close associations with the Great Western, sharing common directors and in many cases the lines, such as the Bristol & Exeter Railway, the South Devon Railway and the Cornwall Railway were surveyed and constructed by Brunel. Though independent, many of these lines were operated by the Great Western, with Great Western locomotives and rolling stock but in time all were either merged with or bought by the Great Western.

As the table shows the earliest lines were incorporated shortly after the Great Western and constructed at the same time so once the Great Western opened from London to Bristol in 1841 it was already possible to carry on the journey to Bridgewater via the Bristol & Exeter Railway.

Many lines incorporated in the early 1840s were part of the first Railway Mania, a speculative frenzy in the railway shares of newly promoted lines. When the Mania reached its zenith in 1846 no fewer than 272 Acts of Parliament had been passed authorising almost 9,500 miles of new railways. Around a third of these authorised lines were never built following the inevitable collapse of this boom and bust bubble. But unlike the 17th Century "Tulip Mania" or stock market bubbles, Railway Mania did leave behind some tangible benefits: a vast and economically useful expansion of the British railway system, though perhaps at an inflated cost.

Railway Company	Act of Incorporation	Date opened	Track Gauge	Date purchased or merged with GWR
Bristol and Exeter Railway	1836	1841	Broad	1876
Cheltenham and Great Western Union Railway	1836	1841	Broad	1843
Bristol & Gloucester Railway	1839	1844	Broad	Bought by Midland Railway 1846
Oxford Railway	1843	1844	Broad	1844
South Devon Railway	1844	1846	Broad	1876
Berks & Hants Railway	1845	1847	Broad	1845
Cornwall Railway	1846	1859	Broad	1889
West Cornwall Railway	1846	1852	Broad	1878

These independent lines connecting to the Great Western Railway were loyal to Brunel's broad gauge vision and during the 1840s and 50s the Great Western's own expansion to South and West Wales and the Midlands were also built to the broad gauge.

But look at the short lived history of the Bristol and Gloucester Railway as an independent line to see the maggot eating out the heart of the glossy broad gauge apple. Built as a broad gauge line, the Bristol and Gloucester connected Bristol to Gloucester and then Cheltenham. From Gloucester, travellers could reach Birmingham, via Cheltenham, on the Birmingham and Gloucester Railway. This, though, was a standard gauge railway so at Gloucester station, travellers from the South-West to the Midlands had to decamp from their broad gauge carriages and cross the platform for a standard gauge train. The Bristol and Gloucester and Birmingham and Gloucester shared running rights over mixed gauge track from Gloucester to Cheltenham and in 1844 the two companies merged to form the short lived Birmingham & Bristol Railway, acquired just two years later in 1846 by the Midland Railway.

This gave the Midland Railway access into Great Western territory and by 1854 the line all the way through to Gloucester had been converted to standard gauge.

During the 1840s and 50s many small railway companies merged with or were acquired by companies such as the Great Western Railway, Midland Railway and London and North Western Railway. Eager for access to rich freight and passenger opportunities these growing companies eyed covetously

Above:
*Maidenhead
Bridge*

the territory of their rivals. To resist this type of invasion, incumbent companies sometimes invested in lines with initially poor economic prospects simply to block encroachment by their competitors. Promoted by the Great Western, the Berks & Hants Railway, for example, with branches from the Great Western mainline at Reading to Hungerford in Berkshire and Basingstoke in Hampshire was built simply to thwart the London & South Western Railway's ambitions in those counties.

As we saw, the Great Western was out manoeuvred by the Midland Railway in its initial foray to Birmingham from Bristol via Gloucester. It was, though, able to reach Birmingham and Wolverhampton in the early 1850s by building its Birmingham and Oxford Junction Railway. By now the Great Western was extending into territory dominated by standard gauge track and though the first section, Oxford to Banbury, opened in 1850, was built as a broad gauge line the second section from Banbury to Birmingham and opened in 1852 was built with mixed gauge track.

Above: *Rain, Steam & Speed: The Great Western Railway J M W Turner's masterpiece first exhibited in 1844*

Mixed, broad and standard gauge, track never got any further north than Wolverhampton and the remainder of railways built or acquired in the West Midlands and North-West by the Great Western were all standard gauge.

By the 1880s the 500 miles of broad gauge track operated by the Great Western was miniscule by comparison with the nation's almost 13,000 miles of standard gauge track. The difficulties of building and operating mixed gauge track and building convertible gauge stock had become increasingly

untenable and from the 1850s the GWR had started a piecemeal conversion of broad gauge to mixed gauge while the straight conversion from broad to standard gauge started in 1866. By 1869 broad gauge trains had ceased to run north of Oxford while Wales saw its last working in 1872. By 1873, 200 miles of branch lines in Berkshire, Wiltshire, Hampshire and Somerset had been quietly converted.

As Chairman Gooch had encouraged the conversion to standard gauge but there was perhaps reluctance to remove

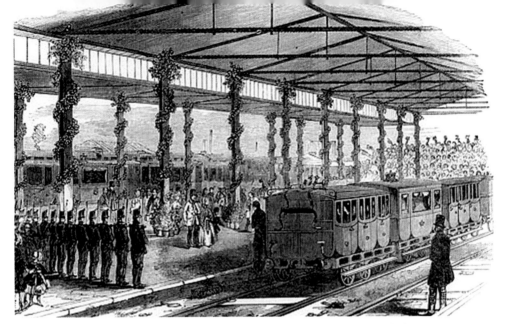

Above: *Queen Victoria changing trains at Gloucester 1849*

the remaining 177 miles from London to Bristol, Exeter and Plymouth while he was still alive. With his death in 1889 conversion of those final miles shifted from being a pressing consideration to one that required a plan of action.

Using the experience gained to date the final conversion was planned in meticulous detail which included a 50 page manual of instructions together with a further 30 pages for the superintendents of the Bristol and Exeter divisions.

At daybreak on Saturday 21 May 1892 over 4,200 platelayers and gangers were assembled along the line ready for the task. All broad gauge rolling stock and non-essential engines had already been worked to Swindon where miles of specially prepared sidings were filled with an astounding and overwhelming array of broad gauge rolling stock and locomotives.

Strictly to plan the conversion was completed by 4:00am on the Monday morning so that in less than two days 177 route miles had been converted from broad to "narrow" gauge with the minimum interruption to traffic.

Travelling West

Travelling West

Opposite: *East Pool tin mine's preserved engine house*

Many people's image of the Great Western is a nostalgic one, conjured up by its role as a "holiday" line carrying passengers to idyllic seaside resorts in South Devon and the far west of Cornwall. An image encapsulated by countless shots of copper capped steam engines heading passenger trains along the picturesque seawall from Dawlish to Teignmouth and an image carefully fostered today by steam heritage railways such as the Dartmouth Steam Railway and the South Devon Railway.

In some respects the heritage railway's lovingly preserved and somewhat sanitised image is false. A quick glance at rail route maps of the Great Western during its independent existence, at the time of Grouping, say, or just before Nationalisation in 1948, will confirm its most dense rail systems were round the industrial heartlands of South Wales, the West Midlands and the North West.

And long before holidays were invented freight was important in the West Country too, with extensive mineral and agricultural traffic and connection to the active harbours and docks of Plymouth, Falmouth and Penzance.

As early as 1826 business interests in Plymouth had started proposing a railway from Exeter to Plymouth but difficulties of terrain, economics and politics meant that it was not until 1859 that it was possible to travel by rail from Exeter to Penzance.

Extending the railway to Penzance required the agency of several separate independent companies, though each was closely associated with and ultimately absorbed by the Great Western Railway. The main companies involved were the South Devon Railway, the Cornwall Railway and the West Cornwall Railway.

South Devon Railway

Though there had been discussions about linking Exeter and Plymouth by rail since 1826 it took the construction of the Bristol & Exeter Railway (opened 1841) to galvanise local promoters to come up with the first definite scheme in 1840.

From three possible schemes the promoters chose the most direct route across the challenging terrain between Exeter and Plymouth. This 37 mile route would involve a climb to 1,190 feet and require two long tunnels and three rope worked inclines. In spite of these difficult obstacles the scheme was presented to Parliament but never passed beyond the Bill stage and eventually lapsed as schemes following a more level route via Newton Abbot began to gain favour.

Though operating as independent companies, the Great Western and Bristol & Exeter worked closely together in establishing a broad gauge rail network and were referred to as Associated

Companies. The promoters of a new company, the Plymouth, Devonport and Exeter Railway were confident of financial support from the Associated Companies for a broad gauge railway from Exeter to Plymouth via Newton Abbott. This proved correct and the Associated Companies offered £450,000 provided local promoters could match this with a contribution of £500,000. With little Parliamentary dissent an Act for the new company, now renamed the South Devon Railway and with authorised capital of £1.1m, was passed in July 1844.

The Atmospheric Railway decision

As well as financial support from the Associated Companies the South Devon Railway also acquired the services of Isambard Kingdom as surveyor and engineer of the line.

The proposed route followed the coast from Exeter to Newton Abbott but from there needed to cross hilly terrain with steep gradients and sharp curves likely to task the limited power of contemporary steam locomotives. With his febrile mind Brunel could see

the appeal of the ingenious but definitely embryonic idea of atmospheric traction developed by brothers Jacob and Joseph Samada and installed on the Dalkey extension of the Dublin and Kingstown Railway in 1844.

The concept was simple. Stationery steam engines created a vacuum in an iron pipe positioned between the rails of the running track. Once vacuum was created pistons in the pipe attached to carriages above would suck them along at speed.

The benefits claimed for the Samada brothers' patented system which particularly appealed to Brunel were the ability to run trains over steeper gradients and round sharper curves without also having to drag the dead weight of a steam locomotive up a hill. As well as saving construction costs Brunel saw this as a solution to traversing the difficult hilly ground beyond Newton Abbott and took directors and representatives of the South Devon to Ireland to see the Dalkey Railway in action.

Brunel was committed. He wanted the South Devon to be built as an atmospheric railway but the decision needed to be ratified at a shareholder's meeting held on 28th August 1844.. The Chairman was at first disinclined to vote in favour

and one shareholder pointed out that the Dalkey Railway was just two miles long compared to the South Devon's 50 miles but generally there was little objection and the decision was approved, testament again to Brunel's personal magnetism. But not everyone was persuaded. Daniel Gooch, a practical and skilled engineer and the Great Western's Superintendent of Locomotives, is recorded as saying "I could not understand how Mr Brunel could be so misled. He had so much faith in his being able to improve it that he shut his eyes to the consequences of failure."

Building the line

Construction of the Exeter to Newton Abbott section began almost immediately after the atmospheric ratification meeting and contracts were placed for the vacuum pipe and seven pumping houses required for that section of line. Construction was mainly on the level and though two tunnels and extensive rock blasting was required near Teignmouth the line to Teignmouth was opened for conventional loco hauled

Above: *Dawlish Station in the 1870s showing single track broad gauge line and atmospheric pumping station in the background*

trains as soon as May 1846 and extended to Newton Abbott by December 1846. These trains, six a day, were hauled by 2-2-2 broad gauge locomotives hired from the Great Western and continued to run in conjunction with experimental use of the atmospheric system after September 1847. All train services, passenger and freight, were taken over by the atmospheric system from February 1848.

Failure of the atmospheric railway

Initial performance of the atmospheric railway looked compelling, speeds were high and passengers appreciated the lack of noise, smoke and smuts. But soon

operating problems became apparent. Fuel consumption at the pumping stations was greater than expected and much more than that of conventional locomotives, the management of rail crossings, turnouts and level crossings was difficult and resorting to complicated auxiliary pipes to manoeuvre coaches at stations underlined how cumbersome the system was. To those problems was added the continuous challenge of preserving a vacuum in the pipes as the leather seals at the top dried out, cracked, split and suffered from sea water rot.

In May 1848 the company set up a committee to investigate the efficiency of the atmospheric system and in August Brunel delivered a lengthy report resulting

in the directors' decision to suspend atmospheric working. At a cost £431,000, including payment for four never used pumping houses beyond Newton Abbott, the experiment consumed almost half the company's capital, burdening it with financial problems for a number of years and slowing down completion of the route to Plymouth.

Getting to Plymouth

Torquay and Totnes were reached during 1847 and by May 1848 the

line had reached a temporary station at Laira, on the outskirts of Plymouth. The railway's permanent terminus at Plymouth was finally reached in April 1849.

The route from Totnes to Plymouth, with steep gradients, sharp curves and a spectacular viaduct at Ivybridge is still today regarded as "difficult". Some historians contend this is the heritage of a line that was constructed on a route originally planned for an atmospheric railway which, in theory, would have been better suited to those hills and sharp curves.

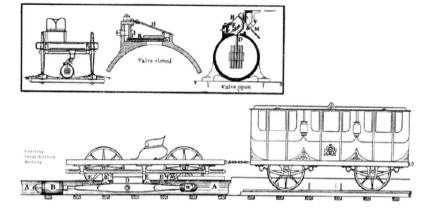

Courtesy,
Great Western
Railway

The West Cornwall Railway

The first railways in West Cornwall provide an interesting insight into the way early railways built for purely local purposes, usually the transport of coal or minerals, were gradually connected to and included in the national rail network.

West Cornwall, with its once intensive mining industry, can boast one of Britain's earliest railways, the 4 foot gauge Redruth and Chasewater which began operating in 1825. This was purely a mineral railway built to carry copper ore to docks on the Fal Estuary and never carried passengers.

Another early mineral railway, but one that carried passengers and eventually became part of the Great Western, was the Hayle Railway. Opened in 1837 this was a classic mineral railway operated by both horses and steam together with four rope operated inclines. Standard gauge, it was built to transport tin and copper from Redruth and Camborne to sea ports at Hayle and Portreath. From 1843 it started carrying passengers on its main line, was absorbed by the West Cornwall Railway in 1852 and is still extant today as the Hayle to Redruth section of the Cornish Mainline.

The West Cornwall Railway was formed by local business interests with the aim of extending the Hayle Railway's eastern end to Penzance and the western end to Truro. The line's engineer was Brunel but early proposals for the Redruth to Truro section to be operated as an

atmospheric railway were soon dropped as the South Devon Railway's problems with this system began to unfold.

The scheme's first Parliamentary Bill in 1845 was defeated but a second bill received Royal Assent in August 1846. This provided for acquisition of the Hayle Railway but also stipulated that the line should be broad gauge. Raising capital and loans for railway investment became much tighter after the 1845 collapse of the first Railway Mania bubble and although the Hayle Railway was acquired in November 1846 the West Cornwall

decided to retain standard gauge for the line from Penzance to Truro. This required variation to the Royal Assent granted in 1846 and deferred construction of the line from Hayle to Penzance until 1850. The variation of Assent came with a sting in the tail: the new powers were conditional upon the West Cornwall laying broad gauge rails on six months' notice from any connecting broad gauge line.

The line from Redruth, on the old Hayle Railway, to Penzance was completed and opened, without ceremony, in March 1852. Meanwhile construction of the eastern section from Redruth to Truro was proceeding well and the opening of Higher Town station on the western margin of Truro on the 25th August 1852 was this time marked with celebrations to acknowledge completion of the route from Penzance to Truro.

The Cornwall Railway

In the 1830s Falmouth was Cornwall's largest population centre with a large port whose reliance on the packet trade was being threatened by Southampton with its closer road and coastal sea connections to London.

Alert to this threat and alarmed by the 1830 proposal to build the London and Southampton Railway local businessmen, like their contemporaries in Bristol, saw their best defence in the construction of a direct railway from Falmouth to London.

Early proposals in the 1830s proposed a line following the old coaching roads through Launceston and Okehampton and then on to Basingstoke or Reading and from there to London. Inevitably this huge undertaking, referred to as the Central Route, failed through lack of

funds.

The London and Southampton Railway (now renamed the London & South Western Railway) link between the cities was opened in 1840. In 1842 the Government announced the transfer of all but South American packet traffic to Southampton. At a stroke this decision wiped out 80% of the putative Falmouth to London Railway's traffic. Undeterred, the Falmouth promoters turned their attention from the Central Route to a Coastal Route via Plymouth and Exeter, now made viable by the Bristol and Exeter Railway and the line being built from Exeter to Plymouth by the South Devon Railway.

In 1843 the Cornwall Railway Committee approached the Great Western Railway and Associated Companies and found them favourable to the idea of a broad gauge connection between the Cornwall Railway and South Devon Railway but without any direct financial assistance being offered.

The Cornwall Railway Cornwall issued a prospectus for investors in 1844 and appointed Captain William Moorson to survey the route. Moorson, a civil engineer with a military background and a mixed reputation: usually a competent

engineer but occasionally guilty of faulty work attributed to his tendency to take on too many commissions.

Assuming the use of the atmospheric system, Moorson's route over the hilly terrain involved sharp curves and his proposal for crossing the Tamar estuary by ferry was particularly impractical. The first Cornwall Railway Bill submitted to Parliament in 1845 failed largely because the proposed route with its steep hills and dangerous curves was regarded as unsafe.

The Railway dismissed Moorson and asked Brunel to resurvey and provide a fresh, safer route for the line. This was completed within three months and a fresh Bill submitted to Parliament in November 1845, ready for the 1846 session. Royal Assent was obtained in August 1846, predicated, though, on the proviso that the Tamar estuary would be crossed by bridge, as proposed by Brunel, instead of by ferry.

Following the collapse of the Railway Mania bubble, funding new railways became increasingly difficult and although the Cornwall Railway

Above: *Crowds throng to meet the first train to Falmouth Station, 1863*

had authorised capital of £1.6m many subscribers failed to meet their calls and had their shares forfeited. Construction work had started around St. Austell but lack of funds saw all further construction work cease between 1848 and 1852. Construction only started again, in 1852, after the company underwent a capital reconstruction and had its borrowings guaranteed by the Great Western and Associated Companies.

To save money and at Brunel's suggestion the line was constructed as a single track railway. The demands of building the Saltash bridge across the Tamar estuary at Saltash and 37 viaducts across the valleys between Plymouth to Truro meant that the line was not opened until 1859, the date clearly shown on the piers of the single track bridge, named the Royal Albert Bridge when opened by Prince Albert at a special ceremony on 2nd May 1859.

Completion of the line meant it was now possible to travel by train from London to Penzance but with a change of gauge from the Cornwall Railway to the West Cornwall Railway at Truro.

Falmouth at last

Connecting Falmouth by rail was always the Cornwall Railway promoters' main aim but as the first contractor appointed to build the line had gone bankrupt the railway had to turn again to the Great Western and Associated Companies for assistance. This was forthcoming, but at a price: the company had to yield a 1,000 year lease of their line to the Associated Companies, an arrangement authorised by Act of Parliament in 1861. Management of the railway was now in the hands of a Joint Committee of Management made up of four Cornwall Railway directors, three South Devon directors, three Bristol & Exeter directors and two directors from the Great Western.

The extension to Falmouth was completed and opened in 1863 and in 1864 a steeply graded connection was made to the Falmouth Dock Company's own railway system.

Now referred to as the Maritime Line the Truro to Falmouth railway has always been operated as a branch line and has remained a single track railway to the present day.

The Great Western takes over

In the curious piecemeal way that the railway had been connected to Penzance there was the anomaly of the last few miles from Truro to Penzance being standard instead of broad gauge. There was, however a legal provision that enabled the Cornwall Railway to demand that the West Cornwall Railway install broad gauge rails. Each company was as impecunious as the other and the only way the broad could be installed was for each company to surrender its line to the Associated Companies who then went ahead and laid the broad gauge tracks.

The first broad gauge goods trains started running in November 1866 followed by passenger trains in March 1867. It had been a tortuous and long winded task but, finally, after almost two decades, the broad gauge finally reached the western tip of Cornwall.

In 1876 the Associated companies amalgamated with the Great Western which now assumed the leases of the Cornwall and West Cornwall railways. Control of the line was now undertaken by a Joint Committee of Management with four Great Western directors and four from the Cornwall railways.

The First Train Services

The first railway companies were local affairs designed specifically to increase the efficiency and lower the cost of transporting goods and freight, such as coal in the case of the Stockton & Darlington and minerals on Cornwall's Hayle Railway. Transporting passengers was initially a secondary consideration though as soon as it opened the operators of the Liverpool and Manchester Railway were immediately surprised at the overwhelming demand of passengers wanting to travel on their new railway

Brunel, who made a point of visiting and viewing engineering developments around Britain, had travelled as a passenger on the Liverpool & Manchester in 1831. Although at that date he had not been involved in any railway development or construction, his diaries confirm that he had a vision, what he referred to as one of his "castles in the sky", of transporting passengers both more quickly and more comfortably than on the Liverpool & Manchester.

When appointed engineer of the Great Western Railway he was able to articulate this vision and was able also to persuade the directors that building broad gauge track was right for a company that was going to prioritise on the speed and comfort of passengers.

The choice of broad gauge and emphasis on passenger traffic may have signalled the Great Western as radically different from other railway companies of the time but when it came to the class apartheid that characterised the early Victorian era the Great Western was just as conventional as the rest, dividing its travellers into First, Second and Third Class passengers.

Above: *Great Western open third class passenger truck*

Class division

In the early 19th Century the working classes made up almost 90% of the population and were regarded with some fear as "the mob" by the upper and middle classes. These franchised classes had as little to do with the mob as possible, a segregation reinforced by the railways' passenger class division.

On the Great Western passenger trains consisted of first and second class carriages, covered coaches offering considerable comfort, particularly in first class. Third class travel, consisting of wooden benches in open trucks with holes drilled in the floor to let out rainwater, was, by contrast, uncomfortable and rudimentary. The Great Western did not even grace these wagons with the term "carriage" and described them in their stocklists as "trucks".

And like trucks they only ran in goods trains, what the early railways called "baggage" trains, for the first few years of the 1840s, taking over 9 uncomfortable hours from London to Bristol. It looks almost as though the Great Western and its railway contemporaries were trying to discourage travel by the poorest and lowest of the land. The railways might,

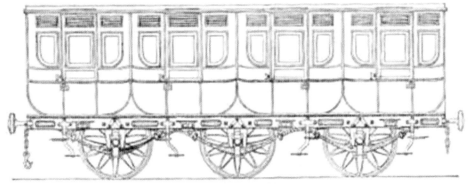

First Class carriage

arguably, have been built for the masses, but the masses, it was thought, could not afford to or even have a need to travel.

Travelling comfort

Taking advantage of the broad gauge the Great Western quickly discarded four wheel carriages in favour of six wheel underframes. In a 24 foot long first class coaches each of the four 6 foot by 9 foot compartments could comfortably seat eight passengers. As well as being generously proportioned these compartments were sumptuously appointed with well-padded and upholstered seats with buttoned backs and armrests.

From the start and for the first 10 or 15 years first class carriage design closely reflected the style of road and mail coaches with curved body panels and rounded tri-corner windows on either side of the doors.

Second class carriages, though covered, had no windows, just open sides vulnerable to wind and rain. Inside, up to 72 passengers could be accommodated on extremely cramped wooden benches. The replica second class coach illustrated gives a good idea of the utilitarian style.

Disaster in the Sonning Cutting

Today, with our awareness of health and safety, passengers travelling in open trucks just seems like an accident waiting to happen. And it duly did: within just six months of the railway

opening the route from London to Bristol.

The Sonning Cutting accident happened in the early hours of Christmas Eve, 1841. A Great Western goods train made up of three third class passenger trucks marshalled between engine and tender and some heavily laden goods wagons had left Paddington at 4:30 am, arriving at the Sonning Cutting, near Reading just before 7:00 am.

There had been recent heavy rain and shortly before the arrival of the goods train a landslip from the steep sides of the cutting had dumped two to three foot of soil onto the track. Unseen by the driver in the dark December morning, the engine, *Hecla*, ploughed into it, was de–railed and came to sudden stop. First reports of the accident which described the 38 passengers on the train as being "chiefly of the poorer class" were recorded in the Times on Christmas Day and stated that following derailment of the engine and tender

"...the next truck, which contained the passengers, was thrown athwart the line, and in an instant was overwhelmed by the trucks behind, which were thrown into the air by the violence of the collision, and fell with fearful force upon it".

Above: *Thomas Cook's first railway excursion from Leicester to Loughborough in 1841*

Eight passengers died at the scene and 17 were seriously injured, one of whom died in hospital six days later.

Incidents such as this and ongoing political pressure eventually saw a Board of Trade investigation and in November 1844 Sir Robert Peel's Conservative government introduced the Railway Regulation Act. Designed partly to encourage greater travel by the poor in search of employment in Britain's burgeoning industrial centres, the Act stipulated that railway companies must provide enclosed third class accommodation and run at least one train a day conveying third class passengers at an average speed of not less than 12 mph, including stops at all stations, with fares of no more than 1d a mile. To soften the introduction of the Act and as a concession, the railway companies were exempted from paying passenger duty on these trains.

Cheap outings for the working classes

Until the late 1860s most passenger revenue on the Great Western came from second class travellers but after this date receipts were dominated by the growth of third class travellers so that by 1912 second class facilities were withdrawn, leaving the railway with just two classes of travel, 1st and 3rd.

One way in which the working classes became familiar with the idea of rail travel was the introduction of rail excursions. Although rail companies had run limited excursion trains in the 1830s the first true precursor of these tours is generally regarded as Thomas Cook's outing on Sunday, 5th July 1841, when he transported 540 campaigners from Leicester to a Temperance Rally at Loughborough. The rest, as they say, is history and the expansion of Thomas Cook's excursion agency business laid the foundations for the development of a global travel business.

Other excursion agents, social entrepreneurs just like Cook, encouraged the rapid growth of the business during the 1840's when the site of "monster" excursions, three engines hauling trains of a thousand passengers or more, became a common sight. The Great Western was quite late in embracing the concept rail excursions, not running its first until 1849 but engaging with the idea in time to capitalise on the huge demand for excursions to the Great Exhibition of 1851.

The expansion of excursion traffic coincided with the slowly growing concept of holidays, linked initially to Saturday half-days and though some were solely concerned with pleasurable outings such as a trip from London to the seaside at Brighton, many were organised for very respectable institutions. Excursion Agents typically organised tours for Sunday Schools, Mechanics' Institutes, Temperance Societies and enlightened employers.

No doubt drunkenness would have been evidenced on some outings but as well as improving the mobility of the working classes and introducing them to open places, allowing them to mingle on railways and at stations with their so-called "betters" would have gone some way to softening the harsh class division and fear of the "mob" that existed in the early years of the 19th Century.

The painting of Paddington Station

Above: *Exchange clock at Bristol with two minute hands displaying both railway time and local mean time*

in 1859 by the popular, populist even, painter William Frith Powell provides a very good picture of travel on the Great Western. As the main focus of the picture is the people, over 100 of them, some even identifiable by name, we get a good impression of the social mix of passengers travelling on the Great Western at the end of the 1850s. True, there are no barefoot urchins or grimy toshers but at the far right of the picture two top hatted detectives, Haydon & Brett, well known to the Victorian public and about to arrest their fleeing suspect, do leave a sense, at least, that all life is here.

Broad gauge was the fastest

The period from 1844, when difficulties of trans-shipment from broad to standard gauge at Gloucester and elsewhere aroused public complaint, through to the end of the 1840s is referred to in British railway history as the "Gauge War". The "War" was defined by vigorous debate in newspapers and pamphlets, government committees, an Act of Parliament and even a competition proposed by Brunel between broad and standard gauge locomotives.

Brunel's proposal for the competition was made to the Royal Commission appointed in 1845 to consider and report on the gauge problem. The Commissioners agreed to the competition and the tests were arranged between Brunel and G.P.Bidder a fellow railway engineer and close friend of Robert Stephenson. On the broad gauge runs were made between Paddington and Didcot with *Ixion*, one of Gooch's 2-2-2 Firefly class locomotives. For the standard gauge Bidder selected one of Stephenson's newest locomotives, referred to simply as "Engine A".

Significantly heavier loads and more consistent overall performance by *Ixion* provided a compelling broad gauge victory. Comparable figures from other railways at the time also underline the superiority of Great Western performance.

Railway	Total annual loco miles	Average weight of trains		Average speed of passenger trains
		Passenger	Goods	
	000 miles	Tons	Tons	mph
London & Birmingham	1,415	42.4	162	20.0
Grand Junction	870	43.5	152	20.8
South Western	743	36.0	121	24.0
Great Western	1,623	67.0	265	27.5

Table source: The Great Western Railway, David & Charles 1984

Clearly the Great Western was carrying the heaviest loads and at the highest average speeds. But the comparative advantage was quickly eroded as the construction of standard gauge track improved, particularly as timber sleepers replaced the old stone blocks, and better engineering technology produced more powerful locomotives.

The Broad Gauge Locomotives

For the first 30 years of its existence the Great Western's senior management rested almost entirely on four men, Charles Russell the Chairman, Charles Saunders fulfilling roles as Company Secretary and General Manager, Brunel, who remained Company engineer until his death in 1859, and Daniel Gooch.

Both the timing and manner of Gooch's appointment as Chief Locomotive Assistant in 1837 proved fortuitous. The Great Western's first locomotives, delivered by outside contractors from 1837 onwards but built to Brunel's careful specification, proved, in operation, to be almost universally feeble.

Quickly demonstrating his skills as a practical engineer and by working with and reviewing the performance of the best engines in the railway's motley collection Gooch was able by 1840 to deliver *Firefly*, the first engine of his own design and the first engine of a famous class of 2-2-2 passenger locomotives.

Taking advantage of the broad gauge Gooch was able to go on and develop powerful, fast engines best defined by his single wheeler 4-2-2 *Iron Duke* Class of 1847. Capable of speeds up to 80 mph these were at the time Britain's fastest express passenger locomotives.

With the ultimate demise of the broad gauge apparent from as early as the 1850s and with a rapidly expanding standard gauge network Great Western locomotive development became more focused on standard gauge engines. Though the Iron Dukes represented the cutting edge of locomotive development in the 1840s by the 1890s their visually similar successors, the Rovers, had a distinctly archaic appearance.

Look at pictures of broad gauge engines in the 1880s and beginning of the 1890s. The old fashioned express engines, cumbersome looking saddle tanks and those odd hybrids, "narrow" gauge engines converted to broad gauge ready to be converted back to standard gauge, already look anachronistic, like a race of locomotives from an earlier era squeezed to the western edge of the network and destined for extinction. An extinction eloquently captured in the photos of broad gauge graveyards, row upon row of engines waiting silently to be scrapped.

Brunel's locomotives

Brunel is rightly remembered as one of Britain's most successful engineers. But in a career that embraced an astounding range of disciplines, tunnelling, bridge building, railway construction, locomotives and shipbuilding, there were, inevitably some failures. Some historians have used his failures to unfairly diminish his greatness, claiming, somewhat cynically, that Brunel boasted his successes were all

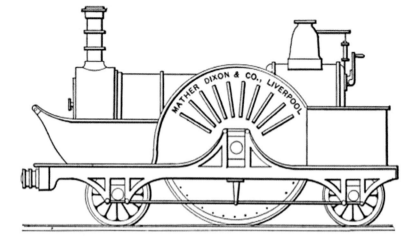

his own work while his failures were the fault of third party contractors.

All the Great Western's first engines were delivered by outside contractors but the specification and design were largely Brunel's own work.

From 1837 onwards and working to Brunel's specification, three contractors, Mather Dixon, Sharp Roberts, Charles Tayleur and Robert Stephenson & Co, delivered 13 more or less conventional 2-2-2 tender engines. *Aoelus*, the second engine delivered from Charles Tayleur's Vulcan Foundry headed the inaugural train from London to Maidstone Bridge on the 4th June 1838.

Newly appointed and familiar with the engines of Robert Stephenson, Gooch persuaded Brunel to buy two standard gauge engines from Robert Stephenson and have them converted to broad gauge. The two engines were available from an order cancelled by the New Orleans Railway and the first one, *North Star*, was delivered in November 1837. *North Star* quickly demonstrated its superiority to all the other 2-2-2s ordered by Brunel and provided the basis for the design and development of Gooch's own Firefly class of engines.

A further four other engines were distinctly unconventional, their use of geared mechanisms clearly bearing the hallmark of Brunel's fertile imagination. The first two, *Snake* and *Viper* were delivered from Haigh Foundry in 1838. In line with Brunel's specifications they had driving wheels geared to a 2:3 ratio

in order to keep piston stroke speed low while allowing high track speed. Within a couple of years both engines had been rebuilt with a conventional drive and after conversion to tank engines for use on the South Devon Railway had surprisingly long lives, surviving in use until the end of the 1860s.

The other two geared engines, also delivered in 1838 and built by R W Hawthorne & Co, were *Thunderer* and the heroically massive *Hurricane* with its 10 foot driving wheels. Both engines made use of engineer Thomas Harrison's patent for locomotive boilers and engine mechanisms to be supported on separate units. Harrison, later a superintending engineer on the North Eastern Railway, is sometimes credited with the design of these engines though it seems clear the gearing arrangements were entirely attributable to Brunel.

Though there were wild but unproven claims of *Thunderer* attaining a speed of 100mph both engines had been withdrawn and scrapped within two years, confirming, more accurately, their status as experimental failures.

Daniel Gooch (1816 – 1889)

In July 1837, while working at Robert Stephenson & Co's Warrington works, Gooch wrote to Brunel seeking a position on the Great Western Railway. They met a few weeks later in August 1837 and Brunel, impressed by the young Gooch, still only 21, straightway recommended to the company's directors his appointment as Chief Locomotive Assistant. Gooch started work almost immediately and was ready to manage delivery of the locomotives ordered by Brunel, the first of which began arriving in November 1837.

Above: *Hurricane. Unconventional and unsuccesful*

History confirms this apparently spur of the moment decision was one of serendipitous good fortune for Brunel. As Brunel's engines began to arrive it quickly became clear that, for all his great gifts, he was a less than outstanding locomotive engineer. Gooch, with an already varied practical engineering background, including an apprenticeship served at Robert Stephenson & Co's Newcastle Works, quickly assessed the engines and was soon able to identify *North Star*, the first engine delivered from Robert Stephenson & Co, as the best of a pretty poor bunch.

Gooch was born in Bedlington, Northumberland where his father was an ironfounder at the Bedlington Iron Works, manufacturers of iron rails for the Stockton & Darlington Railway. As a child it was Gooch's delight to wander among the machinery of the Works and

George Stephenson frequently visited his father at the family home. Having completed his engineering apprenticeship and while still a teenager Gooch moved with his family to South Wales where his father had been appointed to a managerial post at the Tredegar Ironworks where Gooch also worked and continued to gain practical engineering experience. Later in life he recorded in his diaries "I look back upon the time spent at Tredegar as by far the most important years of my life... large works of this kind are by far the best school for a young engineer".

Brunel and Gooch had a very close working relationship and from Gooch's diaries it is clear that although he had enormous admiration for Brunel he was equally aware of his human failings. A particular weakness of Brunel was the utmost faith in his own abilities compared

to others and a belief that if you wanted a job doing well you had to do it yourself. He found it very hard to have trust and confidence in his subordinates and associates.

Brunel must have found the failure of his own locomotive designs particularly chastening, particularly when it quickly became apparent that Gooch was a much more successful and competent locomotive engineer than him. Recognising this, though, Brunel soon granted Gooch almost total autonomy over the management of the company's locomotives, demonstrating for once his complete trust in Gooch, now promoted to the title Superintendent of the Locomotive Department.

To keep them running, the first locomotives delivered to the Great Western required constant maintenance. Both Brunel and Gooch agreed that as the locomotive fleet expanded the railway would need to establish a permanent locomotive facility, capable of repairing, overhauling and eventually building engines. Gooch gave considerable thought to the location for the new

Right: *Sir Daniel Gooch by Leslie Ward 1882*

in many ways, a private man who tended to adopt a rather aloof manner when dealing with associates and subordinates, even men such as Gooch with whom he worked closely for over 20 years until his premature death in 1859. But it's equally clear that Brunel and Gooch had developed a good working relationship based on mutual respect and admiration and on Brunel's death Gooch, who described him as "my oldest and best friend" famously wrote "By his death the greatest of British engineers was lost; the man of the greatest originality of thought and power of execution, bold in his plans, but right."

Works and eventually wrote to Brunel in September 1840 setting out in some detail the pros and cons of building on a green field site near the village of Swindon. Shortly afterwards, as Gooch records in his diary "Mr Brunel and I went to look at the ground, then only green fields, and he agreed with me as to its being the best place." Beyond securing the directors' approval for the proposal Brunel had little further involvement in the construction of Swindon, ample demonstration of his total trust in Gooch.

The diaries of Gooch and other contemporaries suggest that Brunel was,

By the time of Brunel's death Gooch, now a director of the Great Western had complete control of Swindon. He was responsible for the planning, tooling and management of Swindon and had direct control over the locomotives, tenders, rolling stock and rails manufactured there. During the 1860s his overall level of control generated considerable criticism from other board members, suspicious about Gooch's close association with suppliers to the Great Western and the potential for conflicts of Interest. Their particular concern was Ruabon Coal, supplier of coal to the Great Western and a company of which Gooch was chairman, having invested £20,000 in 1856.

His particular nemesis was the company's new chairman, Richard Potter, appointed in 1863 and by September 1864 sustained criticism of Gooch forced his resignation. What, today, we would probably describe as constructive dismissal.

As a prominent engineer and successful businessman the loss of income from the Great Western, £1,500 a year, was probably of little concern to Gooch. In 1860 he had begun a set of associations that made full use of his talents in engineering, finance and organisation to establish, by 1866, telegraphic communication between Britain and the United States. As a member of the boards of the three companies involved, the Great Eastern Steamship Company, the Telegraphic Constructions and Maintenance Company and the Anglo-American Telegraph Company, he was able to co-ordinate the entire enterprise. Importantly, he was able to rescue Brunel's final great venture, the building of the *Great Eastern* steamship, from total ignominy by using the ship to lay the first Atlantic cables. The creation of Gooch as a baronet in 1866 was primarily a reward

for the successful establishment of cross-Atlantic telegraphic communication.

From relatively humble beginnings Gooch had now entered the realms of "the great and the good" and in 1865 entered parliament as the Conservative MP for Cricklade, Wiltshire, a seat he held for the next 20 years.

After the bursting of the second railway mania bubble in 1848 railway companies struggled financially during the 1850s and early 1860s with an ongoing fall in new investment and a significant cut in annual dividends. At the Great Western, where these problems were compounded by the additional costs of maintaining a network of two separate gauges, the company's financial state was particularly parlous with some of the directors fearing impending bankruptcy. When Gooch's old adversary, Chairman Richard Potter, resigned in 1865 to devote more time to his private affairs, the company made a plea to Gooch and he was duly appointed as the Great Western's new Chairman.

The company's share and debenture values had collapsed and taking hold of the situation Gooch's austerity measures included postponement of capital projects, cuts to the quality of train services and a reduction in the number

of the company's directors. By 1872 there was sufficient financial recovery to restore an ordinary dividend of 6% and to begin investment in the Severn Tunnel scheme in which Gooch took a special interest.

Though difficult to determine how important Gooch's role was in the company's recovery it is clear from his letters that he was a very active chairman and his obituary in the Times confirms the view that he had been the saviour of the company, describing it at his death as *"as one of the most compact and prosperous of*

English railways".

Gooch remained chairman of the Great Western until his death in 1889 at the age of 73. He was married twice and had six children, four sons and two daughters, by his first wife Margaret, who died in 1868. His second wife, Emily, whom he married in 1870, outlived him, dying in 1901.

A rich man at his death, Gooch left an estate valued at around £750,000; £50 million in today's terms and significantly more than the estate of £90,000 left by Brunel, his old colleague and mentor.

Gooch's broad gauge locomotives

Gooch rightly deserves the status as the first of the great railway company locomotive engineers. Between 1840 and 1842 the Great Western built 102 six wheeled tender engines to Gooch's own design. Of these, 62 were 2-2-2 express passenger engines with 7 foot driving wheels developed from *North Star* and demonstrating the first standardisation on an extensive scale by any railway.

As a practical, engineer Gooch was no stranger to the footplate, famously driving Firefly class engine *Phlegethon* for Queen Victoria's first ever railway journey from Slough to Paddington on the 13th June 1842. On another special occasion, the opening throughout of the Bristol and Exeter Railway on 1st May 1844, Gooch drove Firefly class engine *Orion,* hauling the train of invited guests the 194 miles from London to Exeter in five hours, a remarkable average speed of 39mph. And then he drove the same engine back to London in even less time, four hours 40 minutes: an incredible record for both engine and driver.

Gooch had already demonstrated his hands-on skill with the improvements

Above: *Daniel Gooch*

he made to *North Star;* largely by making changes to the blast pipe to improve the engine's steaming. Originally one of a pair of engines, *North Star* was built and shipped to the USA for use on the New Orleans Railway but when that company was unable to pay the engines were shipped back to Britain. Sold to the Great Western and converted to broad gauge the engine soon proved itself the best engine from the variety of 2-2-2s delivered from a range of different contractors. *North Star's* sister engine from the New Orleans Railway

Above:

Hirondelle. Built in 1848 this was the 10th engine of the Iron Duke class

order was delivered over a year later and named *Morning Star*. Modified and improved, the two engines provided the basis for a further 10 Star class locomotives delivered from Robert Stephenson & Co between 1839 and 1841.

Having served his apprenticeship and then worked at Robert Stephenson & Co Gooch probably felt comfortable working with the mechanical layout of these engines. Some historians have even suggested he may have been involved in the original design. In any event Gooch used *North Star* as the basis for his first Great Western design, *Firefly* delivered from James, Turner & Evans in March 1840. Essentially similar to *North Star*, a 2-2-2 express passenger engine, but with a bigger boiler and improved front end, *Firefly* was the doyenne of a class that eventually grew to 62 engines.

North Star remained in service until 1871 but was stored at Swindon along with 4-2-2 express *Lord of the Isles*, recognition, perhaps, of their historical status until surprisingly both were scrapped in 1906 because of "lack of space". A replica of *North Star*, using some parts from the original, was built in 1923 ready for the Locomotive Cavalcade of 1925 and can now be seen at the Swindon Steam Railway Museum.

Between March 1840 and December 1842 a further 61 Firefly class locomotives were delivered by a variety of small locomotive builders, their names long since forgotten as they were subsumed into larger enterprises.

1846 was a milestone year for the Great Western with the completion of Swindon Works and the production of its first engine, appropriately named *Great Western*.

Great Western, a 2-2-2 passenger

Above: *Nemesis at Trowbridge. One of Gooch's Ariadne class "Standard Goods"*

engine, with its massive 8 foot driving wheel was a beefed up version of Gooch's Firefly class. Trials of this first engine, no doubt with Gooch on the footplate, saw the early conversion of the engine to a 4-2-2 wheel arrangement with the closely spaced leading wheels set rigidly within the sandwich frames rather than as a separate bogie.

The second and third 4-2-2 engines, *Great Britain* and *Iron Duke*, were built in 1847 with *Iron Duke* establishing the name for this new class with the distinctive look that persisted right up to the demise of broad gauge in 1892.

With an estimated top speed of 80 mph the Iron Dukes affirmed Brunel and Gooch's belief that the broad gauge would permit the construction of the fastest and most powerful engines. Hauled by Iron Dukes, the Great Western's *Flying Dutchman* express from Paddington to Exeter with a journey time of less than four hours remained for several decades the world's fastest train.

In May 1870 three engines of the class, *Great Britain, Prometheus and Estaffete*, were extensively rebuilt with new frames and boilers by Gooch's successor Joseph Armstrong. Further new engines were built with similar specifications between 1871 and 1888 and were referred to as the Rover class. The Iron Dukes were progressively withdrawn between 1870

and 1884 with *Lord of the Isles* being the last engine withdrawn. The Rover class engines continued in service right up to the end of broad gauge in 1892.

Fast express engines always attract the attention of schoolboy train spotters but Gooch was also responsible for the design of the freight, mixed traffic and shunting engines required by the Great Western. Engines such as 0-6-0s of the Caliph and Ariadne classes, usually referred to as Gooch's Standard Goods, mixed traffic 2-4-0s and a series of 4-4-0 saddle tanks specially designed for the sharp curves of the South Devon Railway and which, until the end of broad gauge, remained a distinctive feature of Devon and Cornwall's railways.

Looking quite different from other railways 4-4-0s, the South Devon Railway saddletanks only had frames running back from the leading flangeless driving wheels to the rear buffer beam while the bogie swivelled in a ball and socket joint riveted to a plate fixed underneath the boiler.

Joseph Armstrong (1816 – 1877)

When Gooch resigned from the Great Western in 1864 his role was taken over by Joseph Armstrong, described as Locomotive, Carriage and Wagon Superintendent because his duties also included responsibility for all rolling stock.

Above: 388 class 0-6-0 No 1205. Built as a standard gauge loco, converted to braod gauge in 1884 and reconverted to standard gauge in 1892

Like Gooch, Armstrong was very much a hands-on practical engineer though he had spent rather more years as an engine driver before graduating through the ranks of foremen and assistant locomotive superintendent.

Born in Bewcastle, Cumberland in 1816, Joseph's family moved to Newburn-on-Tyne in 1824 where his father became a bailiff to the Duke of Northumberland and young Joseph went to the Percy Street Academy in Newcastle, the same private school previously attended by Robert Stephenson.

It's thought that the teenage Armstrong, whose family were acquainted with Timothy Hackwork, Methodist philanthropist, locomotive engineer and first locomotive superintendent of the Stockton & Darlington Railway, gained experience driving engines on that railway before taking up a formal post as an engine driver on the Liverpool & Manchester Railway at the age of 20.

Four years later he moved to a similar post on the Hull & Selby Railway where he was soon promoted to the post of foreman, working closely with that railway's locomotive superintendent, John Gray. Armstrong followed Gray to

THE BROAD GAUGE LOCOMOTIVES

Above: *A rover clas 4-2-2- near the end of the broad gauge era*

responsibility for the locomotives of both companies. The following year, 1854, both companies amalgamated with the Great Western becoming the newly established Northern Division of that railway and using the ex S&BR workshops for the maintenance of the standard gauge locomotives, the first owned by the Great Western.

From 1855 Gooch began designing and building standard gauge locomotives at Swindon and from 1859, having been given considerable autonomy by Gooch, Armstrong started building standard gauge locomotives to his own design from an expanded Wolverhampton works.

When Armstrong moved to Swindon to take over Gooch's duties he left his younger brother, George Armstrong in charge of the Wolverhampton Works, a post he was to retain, as Divisional Locomotive, Carriage and Wagon Superintendent, until his retirement in 1897.

With his brother established at Wolverhampton Joseph Armstrong established quite a dynasty of Armstrong's at the Great Western. Four of his sons served apprenticeships at Swindon with John continuing to work for the company right through to 1916. His eldest son, Thomas, left the Great Western to

Brighton Works in 1845 and there got to know David Joy, another early locomotive designer and inventor of Joy's valve gear.

In 1847 Armstrong's progression up the career ladder saw him appointed as Assistant Locomotive Superintendent to Edward Jeffries on the Shrewsbury and Chester Railway (S& CR), being promoted to Superintendent when Jeffries left in 1853.

In the same year the Shrewsbury and Chester Railway pooled its locomotives with the Shrewsbury and Birmingham Railway, with Armstrong assuming

become an engineering salesman while Irving, the youngest, left to become a Methodist minister, carrying on the family's strong Methodist tradition. Sadly his son Joseph "Young Joe", identified as the most able apprentice and engineer, committed suicide at the age of 32, overwhelmed, apparently, by debts of £500 which he hoped to clear with a life assurance policy. George Jackson Churchward, a fellow apprentice and colleague of "Young Joe", acknowledged Joseph's skill when he commented years later that if he hadn't died Joseph, instead of him, would have become William Dean's principal assistant.

Diagnosed with heart problems in 1877 but eager to carry on working Armstrong was persuaded to take a convalescent holiday in Scotland but unfortunately died while travelling north on the 5th June. He was 60.

At Swindon Armstrong had commanded great loyalty and respect from the workforce and at his funeral 2,000 of the Swindon workers together with 100 from Wolverhampton attended the service. With employees and executives from the rest of the Great Western, notables such as William Stroudly and Swindon locals almost 6,000 people crowded into the small churchyard of St Marks, Swindon.

Above: 1076 class 0=6=0 saddletank no 1236, built originally as a broad gauge engine in 1876 and converted to standard gauge in 1892

Above: *Achilles class loco no 3028 preparing to leave Paddington in 1891. This was one of the engines from the 30 strong class originally built for the broad gauge*

After Armstrong's premature death his position was taken over by William Dean, Armstrong's chief assistant at Swindon since 1868. Dean had started his apprenticeship with the Great Western in 1855 at the age of 15, working at the Wolverhampton Works while under the control of Joseph Armstrong.

Joseph Armstrong's broad gauge locomotives

By the time Joseph Armstrong became responsible for the design of broad gauge locomotives the ultimate trajectory of broad gauge was clearly discernible and his output was understandably small, principally 0-6-0 goods engines and saddle tanks with the Rover class of 4-2-2 being the only express passenger and as we've seen this was an updated and improved version

of Gooch's Iron Dukes. With the years spent at Wolverhampton the bulk of Armstrong's legacy was a large number of engines designed and built for the Great Western's standard gauge network.

As the Rover class demonstrates, Armstrong's skill was the development and refinement of established engineering conventions rather than the design of any ground-breaking initiatives. Compared to Gooch, Dean and particularly Churchward the railway literature on Armstrong's locomotives is quite meagre with one historian commenting acidly that this is because there is not a lot to say about them. This is quite unjust. Armstrong was an exceptionally capable and competent engineer as well as being a good manager who on his death bequeathed the Great Western with a better range of reliable engines for every class of traffic than any other railway in Britain.

A good example of Armstrong's unsung competence was his 0-6-0 standard goods engines, the 388 class, lacking the glamour of express passenger locomotives but vital for the Great Western's burgeoning freight traffic.

Cleverly designed as both standard and broad gauge engines, permitting the conversion back to standard gauge following the demise of broad gauge the 388 class finally totalled 310 engines built between 1866 and 1876.

The class were used extensively on passenger trains, not really being supplanted for mixed traffic use until the arrival of Churchward's much more modern 43xx 2-6-0 Moguls in 1911. Withdrawals started in the 1920's as new moguls were delivered in volume and the last members of the class survived until 1934.

Another numerous class of Armstrong locomotives were the 266 0-6-0 double framed saddle tanks of the 1076 class. Built as convertible broad gauge engines between 1870 and 1881 the design was perpetuated by William Dean's 1813 class. The engines proved particularly durable with the remaining survivors soldiering on to 1946.

William Dean (1840 – 1905)

Appointed as Locomotive Superintendent at Swindon following Armstrong's death in 1877, William Dean was the last Great Western engineer to be involved in the design and

building of broad gauge engines but as he was in post during the decline of the broad gauge he is mainly remembered today for his standard gauge designs such as the Dean Goods and the Duke and Bulldog 4-4-0s.

Like his predecessors Gooch and Armstrong, Dean was born into what today we would describe as a middle class family, the second son of Henry Dean, Manager of the Hawes Soap Factory in New Cross, south-east London. Following education at London's Haberdashers Company School and at the age of 15 he began his engineering apprenticeship with the Great Western at the Wolverhampton Stafford Road Works, then under the management of Joseph Armstrong.

Like Armstrong his broad gauge locomotive designs were limited to engines that could be built as broad gauge and then readily converted to standard gauge. But unlike Armstrong he was much more of an experimental engineer, building a number of "one-off" engines, to trial, for example, different boiler designs, centreless bogies and, in 1886, conversion of two 2-4-0 locomotives to compound working.

He is remembered, too, as a great

moderniser, improving the comfort of footplate men with all over cabs and, with a nod to the 20th Century, the introduction of corridor trains and carriages with electric lighting.

There was a degree of sadness in Dean's personal life. He married his first wife in 1865 but she died shortly after the birth of their third child and his second wife, whom he married in 1878, also predeceased him, dying just over 10 years later in 1889.

There has been speculation that these deaths may have affected Dean's health, triggering his resignation from the Great Western at the age of 62 in 1902. Well-liked by the men at Swindon, having maintained the benign paternalism established by both Gooch and Armstrong, they presented him with a chiming grandfather clock which he took to the house provided for him by the company in Folkestone and where he died in 1905.

Though the evidence is unclear, Dean may have been suffering from depression at the time of retirement but there is almost certainly no truth in the myth that he was a "senile old man" who remained the titular head at Swindon while Churchward took over management of the Locomotive Department. Dean's earlier history demonstrated the willingness with which he both encouraged and credited the work of his assistants and the more likely truth is that he was fully aware of the work being done and actively gave Churchward the freedom to develop his own designs.

Dean's broad gauge locomotives

With the emphasis on locomotives for the Great Western's expanding standard gauge network the number of Dean broad gauge designs was quite modest. A small series of 2-2-2 passenger express locomotives, some 2-4-0 tank engines designed for secondary passenger duties and the "one-off" experimental engines already referred to.

Just as with his predecessor Armstrong, Dean's broad gauge designs were constrained by the need to produce locomotives that could be quickly and usefully converted to standard gauge use.

Dean's first broad gauge engines were ten 2-4-0 tank engines, class 3501, built at Swindon in 1885. In 1990 five of the class were rebuilt as 2-4-0 tender engines specifically for working express passenger trains from Exeter to Plymouth. Underlining the "convertibility" of these locos a second batch of ten were built as standard gauge 2-4-0T condensing locomotives. With the end of the broad gauge all ten locomotives were converted as 2-4-0 tender engines and reclassified as class 3201.

These engines were followed in 1887 by the 3521 class of 0-4-2 tanks, 20 built as standard gauge engines and 20 as broad gauge saddle-tanks for use on the South Devon and Cornwall lines. Unsteady running saw both the broad gauge and standard gauge engines converted to an 0-4-4 wheel arrangement and finally, between 1899 and 1902, all the engines, now running as standard gauge, were extensively rebuilt as 4-4-0 tender engines.

Between 1891 and 1892 a class of 30 2-2-2 express passenger engines were built at Swindon, 22 for the standard gauge and 8 for the broad gauge because services still needed to be maintained up to its final demise over a single week-end in 1892. Heavy at the front end and following a derailment in 1893, all 30 engines were rebuilt as 4-2-2s with a front bogie, becoming part of the elegant looking 3031 class of late Victorian single-wheelers.

Expansion
and Acquisition

By 1845 Britain had almost 2,500 miles of railway track, including around 200 miles owned by the Great Western Railway. A cut in interest rates designed to stimulate the economy saw investors switch from the safety of Government bonds to the attraction of potentially much more profitable railway stocks.

This was the start of the Railway Mania, which though over the next decade provided Britain with a useful and functioning rail network also destroyed the savings of many middle class families including such well-known names as Charles Darwin, Charles Babbage, Benjamin Disraeli and the Bronte sisters

In spite of the clamour the amount of new mileage directly sponsored by the Great Western in the second half of the 1840s was actually quite modest though

the company was linked to the promotion of many nominally independent new railway companies eager to connect to the existing Great Western broad gauge. Over the next few decades most of these companies either amalgamated with or were bought by the Great Western.

The Great Western's territorial ambitions in the west Midlands, Wales and north-west also saw it acquiring standard gauge railways during the latter part of the nineteenth century so that by 1900 it had added a further 2,000 miles to its network. By 1923 and including amalgamations in 1922 that anticipated the Railway Grouping these acquisitions provided the Great Western with a network of 3,006 miles. This was the largest of any British company and significantly more than the Great Western's two long term rivals, the London & North Western Railway with

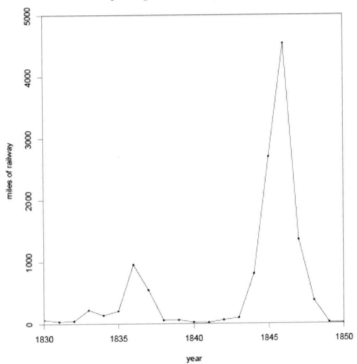

Railway mileage authorized by British Parliament

Left: *Chart source: Andrew Odlyzko - The British Railway Mania of the 1840s*

2,668 miles, and the Midland Railway, a long way behind with just 2,140 miles.

Just another bubble?

There were two distinct phases of railway expansion in the first half of the nineteenth century: one in the 1830s, including important trunk lines such as the Great Western, London &Birmingham and the London & Southampton and the Railway Mania of the 1840s when Parliament authorised almost 5,000 miles of new railways.

The Industrial Revolution had provided a surge in the number of middle class households able to join the burgeoning investor classes. New

Index of British railway share prices

Above: *Chart source: Andrew Odlyzko - The British Railway Mania of the 1840s*

businesses such as railways could now raise capital from affluent and relatively well educated new investors instead of, as previously, relying on banks, wealthy aristocrats and industrialists.

Railway companies became the most aggressive promoters of their own stock, presenting them as virtually risk-free with promised rates of return and annual dividends which with the complacent analysis of hindsight would be seen as unsustainable. To make initial investment even easier the railway companies offered promotional deals which allowed investors to acquire shares with a simple 10% deposit while the company held the right to call on the remaining 90% of the issue price at any time.

The success of railways launched in the earlier 1830s boom coupled with ultimately unrealistic forecasts of future profits saw the start of an irrational fervour for the acquisition of railway shares. The clamour for shares saw their value rise rapidly, peaking in 1845 before collapsing just as quickly by the end of the decade.

Shares in ultimately profitable companies such as the London & North Western Railway collapsed by almost 60% while shares in railways that were promoted but never built became valueless. Almost a third of railway mileage approved by Parliament in 1845 and 1846 was never built. Parliament imposed no limit on the number of railway companies which could be formed by any small group of promoters eager to have their town connected to the rail network. The financial viability of all these new concerns was not a requirement for Parliamentary approval and as many MPs were heavily involved in railway investment most Bills were approved, a clear case of conflict of interest.

A pure economic bubble is irrational exuberance for a product that ultimately has no value. The Dutch Tulip Mania of the seventeenth century, where a single bulb might be worth the annual salary of 10 skilled craftsmen, is a classic example. The 1840s Railway Mania, like the dot. com bubble of 1999 with which it is often compared, is something different. Instead, it spurred the development of Britain's railway system and laid a substantial foundation for the 11,000 miles of network that remains today. With the difficulty of securing the balance of outstanding share calls, finance was a problem for many smaller companies and completion and viability of the lines was often delayed until they were acquired and funded by large well-managed railways such as the Great Western.

Adding to the broad gauge

Of all the new railway proposals submitted to Parliament during the 1845 and 1846 sessions only a handful were sponsored directly by the Great Western. But the company was very supportive of new schemes promoted as broad gauge lines to connect to the existing network of the Great Western

A Railway Crœsus in a fit of dumps —
A call is made — he cannot raise the STUMPS!

Above: *A railway mania investor unable to meet the 90% call*

and its associated companies

Three schemes that were proposed by the Great Western and designed to extend its territory into the Midlands were the Oxford & Rugby Railway, the Birmingham and Oxford Junction Railway and the Birmingham, Wolverhampton & Dudley Railway. These all took advantage of the branch from the Great Western mainline at Didcot to Oxford that had opened in 1844.

Above: *Brunel's tubular iron bridge over the River Wye at Chepstow. A precursor for his famous design of the Royal Albert Bridge crossing the Tamar at Plymouth*

The Birmingham, Wolverhampton & Dudley Railway, running from Wolverhampton to Birmingham Snow Hill and opened in 1854 formed an important link in the Great Western's route from London, Paddington to Birkenhead on the Mersey.

The broad gauge line from Oxford to Banbury was opened in 1850 and upgraded to double track mixed-gauge in 1852. Now that the Great Western was encroaching into Midland Railway territory all the other connecting railways were standard gauge and the section from Banbury to Wolverhampton through Leamington Spa and Birmingham was also constructed to standard gauge instead of broad gauge and opened in 1852. Gauge

conflict had reared its head and as early as 1849 the Great Western had abandoned the Parliamentary sanctioned plans to build a line from Fenny Compton, between Banbury and Leamington Spa, to Rugby because of gauge transhipment problems at Rugby which was already well provided with Midland Railway standard gauge connections to the mixed-gauge track

between Banbury and Wolverhampton.

The Great Western strongly encouraged and supported proposals from other companies submitted to Parliament in 1845 for broad gauge railways that would connect to the Great Western's lines. These included the extensive South Wales Railway and the Berkshire & Hampshire Railway, deliberately planned to block the London & South Western railway encroaching into Great Western territory. In fact, the proposers and providers of capital for the Berkshire & Hampshire Railway were directors of the Great Western and a Parliamentary Act passed in the 1845–46 session saw the railway absorbed into the Great Western.

Extending into South Wales was important for the Great Western, for delivery of coal from the South Wales valleys to London and for access to Fishguard Harbour and Irish ferry services as well as fully developing Brunel's vision of a fast link to New York.

The prospectus for the South Wales Railway was issued in 1844 and proposed a railway running from a junction with the Great Western Railway at Standish, in Gloucestershire, crossing the River Severn on a bridge west of Gloucester and then running through South Wales to Fishguard. The line, engineered by Brunel, would be an important part of the Great Western network and they agreed to provide £600,000 of the £2,400,000 required to build the railway.

Local objections thwarted the initial plans for a bridge crossing the Severn, leaving Brunel to consider two other options: crossing the Severn by ferry or going the long way round via Gloucester. To make the ferry crossing a rail connection from Bristol to the Severn, The Bristol and South Wales Junction Railway, was authorised by Parliament but never built as insufficient capital was raised so the Great Western had to resort to the circuitous route via Gloucester. The extra 18 miles which this route added to the journey from Paddington to South Wales was not resolved until the opening of the Severn rail tunnel in 1886.

The first section of the South Wales Railway, from Chepstow to Swansea was opened in June 1850. Trains to Gloucester started running in July 1852 after completion of Brunel's tubular iron bridge across the River Wye at Chepstow.

During the straitened economic times of the 1850s construction of the line west from Swansea to the Pembrokeshire coast was completed in piece-meal stages with opening of the line to New Milford rather than Fishguard delayed until April 1856.

From opening in 1850 the trains on the South Wales Railway were operated by the Great Western under a lease agreement. An agreement in 1863 saw the Great Western and South Wales Railway merging, adding a further 165 miles to the Great Western's broad gauge network.

Gauge conflict

During the 1840s and 1850s there was great rivalry between the different and rapidly growing railway companies. Each jealously protected their own territory while trying to poach passenger and freight traffic from their rivals' territory.

The two main rivals thwarting the Great Western's expansion into the Midlands and north-west were the Midland Railway and the London & North West Railway. The Midland Railway, formed in 1844 by the amalgamation of three existing companies continued to grow by acquisition under the management of George Hudson so that by 1847 it was valued at £17m and was briefly the world's largest joint-stock company. Styled the "Railway King", George Hudson thrived during the "Wild West" era of the Railway Mania though later had to flee the country, accused of accounting malpractice and fraud involving Ponzi type schemes where capital from new investors was used to pay dividends to existing investors.

In 1846 the Great Western was routed in an early skirmish when the Midland Railway made a surprise purchase of the

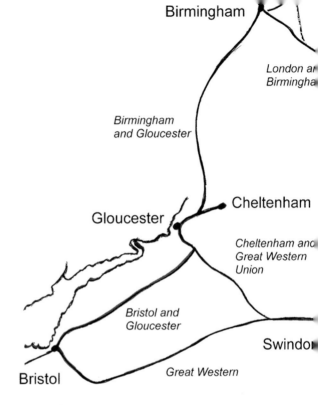

Bristol & Gloucester Railway even as the Great Western was negotiating its own purchase of the line. This was a blow to the Great Western as the Bristol & Gloucester Railway formed an important link in the broad gauge network connecting Bristol to Gloucester, Cheltenham and Swindon.

Above:
Importance of the Bristol & Gloucester Railway to the Great Western's expansion into the Midlands

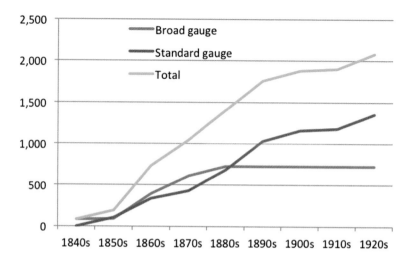

The Midland Railway offered more money than the Great Western was proposing but acceptance of the offer was also dictated by the problems of gauge change the Bristol & Gloucester was experiencing at Gloucester. By 1854 the Bristol and Gloucester had converted from broad gauge to standard gauge.

The standard gauge network was expanding rapidly and it was clear that if the Great Western wanted to extend into the Midlands and northwards it would have to be by standard gauge.

Three companies bought in 1854; the Shrewsbury & Birmingham Railway, the Shrewsbury & Chester Railway and the Shrewsbury, Oswestry & Chester Junction Railway were the Great Western's first standard gauge acquisitions. The engines, rolling stock and 83 miles of track acquired were quickly formed into the Great Western's Northern Division. Crucially, these three railways created a direct connection from London to the north-west through Oxford, Birmingham and Wolverhampton and 1861 saw the first standard gauge direct train from Paddington to Birkenhead.

The next significant acquisition was the West Midland Railway in 1863. The West Midland was already an amalgamation of half a dozen or so smaller companies and provided the Great Western with extensive networks across the Midlands, West Midlands and Wales.

HISTORY OF THE **GREAT WESTERN RAILWAY**

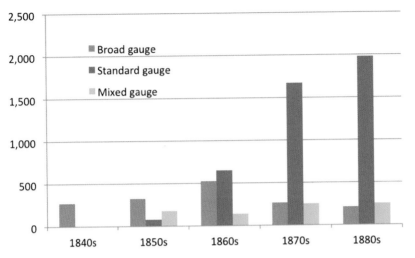

Continuous acquisition

The Great Western continued growing by acquisition from the 1850s right through to the twentieth century. This included amalgamations with long term associates such as the West Cornwall Railway (1866). The Bristol & Exeter Railway (1876), the South Devon Railway (1878) and the Cornwall Railway (1889) as well as tiny railways and branch lines such as the Torbay & Brixham Railway (2 miles) in 1882 and the Minehead Railway (8 miles in 1897)

Just prior to Grouping in 1922 the Great Western had added over 2,000 miles to its network by acquisition and amalgamation. Many of these lines would have been operated by the Great Western from opening so the travelling public would often hqve been unaware of any legal change of ownership.

Histories of the Great Western Railway are often split into two eras, the broad gauge era and the standard gauge era where the broad gauge era is deemed to have lasted until its end in 1892. In reality, though, the broad gauge was in decline from the 1850s. By the 1860's the Great Western already had more miles of mixed and standard gauge track than broad gauge and although over 700 miles was acquired during the second half of the nineteenth century by 1892 early conversion had already whittled this down to less than 250 miles.

Engineering excellence:
The Works

Swindon Locomotive Works

In 1840 Swindon was a small hilltop town surrounded by green fields and a population of only 2,500 people. But by the start of the twentieth century, just 60 years later, it had expanded to accommodate almost 50,000 people, becoming Wiltshire's largest town.

This phenomenal growth was explained by the Great Western's decision in 1840 to site its new purpose built locomotive works in a green field at Swindon next to its London to Bristol mainline. By 1901, with over 14,000 workers and occupying 320 acres, the Works had become the largest industrial complex in Europe and covering 11.25 acres (45,500m²) *A Shop*, the main locomotive fabrication workshop, was one of the world's largest enclosed buildings.

Picking the right green field

Surveying the motley collection of locomotives being delivered to the Great Western from 1837 onwards and conscious of the effort required to keep them running Brunel and Gooch jointly concluded the need for a permanent facility to maintain and repair the railway's engines. Planning for the future and perhaps persuaded, too, by the Grand Junction Railway's plans for a purpose built works at Crewe, the two engineers decided the best solution would be a green field site with plenty of room for expansion.

Charged by Brunel to recommend a site for the railway's principal engine establishment Gooch famously wrote to him on the 13th September 1840 setting out his arguments for the Swindon location. Features dictating his decision were the site was at the junction between the Great Western and the Cheltenham and Great Western Union Railway's line to Cheltenham and Gloucester, the proximity of a canal for delivery of coke and coal and the ease of changing engines and attaching pilot engines to cope with the gradients west of Swindon.

Brunel appears to have accepted Gooch's proposals with little demur and by February 1841 the plans had been rubber-stamped by the Great Western board with construction starting almost immediately afterwards, using stone excavated from the digging of Box Tunnel.

Opening in January 1843 the Works initially consisted of a Running Shed for locomotives on standby, an Engine Shed for servicing locomotives, an Erecting Shop for heavy repairs, a Fitting and Turning Shop, Smiths' Shops as well as a range of small ancillary workshops. The Works was soon employing 400 people including over 70 skilled engineers and from 1843 Brunel began work on a village of 300 terraced cottages to accommodate this new workforce.

Beyond its initial establishment Brunel

Above: *Aeriel view of Swindon showing the roof of A Shop*

had little to do with Swindon and it rarely merits one than one or two pages in his published biographies. Surprising, considering its size and importance to the Great Western Railway but in reality Swindon quickly became the personal fiefdom of Daniel Gooch and he probably deserves more credit than Brunel for its subsequent management and development.

1846 saw delivery of the first new engine entirely constructed at Swindon, one of Gooch's Firefly class built in less than two weeks and provisionally named

Above: *Brunel's Engine House at Swindon with Firefly class loco on the traverser*

Premier but renamed *Great Western* before entering service.

From 1846 Swindon assumed the repair of the railway's carriages and wagons and even began production of track rails. By the early 1860s Gooch's total overall control of Swindon generated criticism from other board members concerned about potential conflict of interest between Gooch and all the third party supply contracts he controlled. Fed up with the constant criticism Gooch resigned in 1864 only to be virtually begged a year later to return as Chairman following the resignation of his chief tormentor and the Great Western's potential bankruptcy.

Over the succeeding decades the Works continued to expand with each subsequent engineer, Joseph Armstrong, William Dean and GJ Churchward responsible for their own distinctive improvements. Armstrong may not be particularly remembered for his locomotive designs but he was a formidable manager of Swindon, responsible for a large new Workshop in 1865, a Carriage Works in 1869 and from 1875 onwards a new locomotive works and foundry.

Both Dean and Churchward continued to expand the Works with Churchward responsible for the opening in 1901 of the previously mentioned

Above: *Brunel's design for the terraced cottages of the Railway Village*

massive *A Shop*.

Development continued through to the twentieth century with C B Collett, Chief Mechanical Engineer from 1921 to 1941, improving both the Work's boiler making facilities and its ability to handle heavy gauge sheet metal.

After nationalisation in 1948 Swindon continued building steam locomotives, both Great Western designs such as Castles and the ubiquitous Pannier tanks and almost 200 of the new British Railways standard classes. Significantly this included *Evening Star,* a 9F 2-10-0 freight locomotive, specially turned out in passenger locomotive livery to celebrate its status as the last steam locomotive built by British Railways.

After nationalisation, each of the regions still had considerable autonomy and in the "dash for diesel" the Western Region made the maverick decision to develop diesel hydraulic engines instead of the diesel electric choice preferred by the other regions. Swindon built a number of the diesel hydraulic Warship and Western class locomotives but when the decision was taken to scrap all these locomotives construction of new engines was centred on Derby and Crewe with Swindon being relegated to the role of heavy repairs and scrapping the redundant steam locomotive fleet.

With the scrapping programme

Above: *A 43xx mogul on the the Swindon Testing Plant in the 1920s*

complete and, post Beeching, a reduction in the amount of rolling stock requiring repair, volume throughput began to dwindle and sections of the Works were progressively closed and demolished. This met the increasing demand for land in the centre of Swindon and in 1986 it was decided to completely close the Works.

Recognising the historical status of the Works a number of the original buildings have been retained and sympathetically restored. One building now houses the Swindon Steam Railway Museum, dedicated to the Works and the Great Western Railway, the old engineers' office is now the headquarters of English Heritage while the remaining buildings have been developed as a "Designer Outlet Village".

The standard gauge works at Wolverhampton

When the Great Western Railway acquired its first standard gauge railway, The Shrewsbury & Birmingham Railway, it also acquired that company's locomotive repair works as well as its very competent Locomotive Superintendent, Joseph Armstrong.

The Great Western quickly expanded the Stafford Road facilities, adding both

broad gauge and standard gauge sheds and works and relegating the old Shrewsbury & Birmingham works to carriage and wagon repairs.

George Armstrong was promoted to Swindon shortly after the Great Western takeover but left his brother, George Armstrong, in charge at Wolverhampton. Under George Armstrong's management Wolverhampton began building new standard gauge locomotives. These were predominantly workhorse engines such as 0-6-0 saddle tanks and 0-4-2 tanks of the 517 class.

With the decline and eventual end of the broad gauge production of standard gauge engines was progressively taken over by Swindon with all new locomotive construction at Wolverhampton ceasing in 1908.

Wolverhampton continued as an important heavy repair facility for the Great Western's northern division and in 1929 the company took advantage of cheap money from the government's Loans & Guarantees ACT to rebuild and substantially upgrade the Stafford Road Works.

The Works continued to repair and overhaul all classes of engine, from humble tank engines to mainline expresses and, after nationalisation, British Railways standard classes until its transfer from the Western Region to the London Midland Region in 1963 followed by almost immediate closure.

Engineering excellence:
The Standard Gauge Locomotives

One of the defining features of British manufacturing during the nineteenth century was the apprenticeship system. Rigorous practical and technical training coupled with active professional institutes provided the engineering excellence that ensured Britain's role as one of world's leading manufacturers.

Most of Britain's railway companies adopted the apprenticeship system and Gooch's well planned Swindon Works, dating back to the 1840s, ensured the Great Western had a ready supply of well qualified and technically gifted engineers.

During the hundred or so years of its independent existence, up to nationalisation in 1948, the Great Western had just six Chief Mechanical Engineers: Gooch, Armstrong, Dean, Churchward, Collett and Hawksworth, all but one of whom had served their apprenticeship with the Great Western. Armstrong, the odd one out, joined the Great Western at the age of 38 when in 1854 the Great Western acquired the Shrewsbury & Birmingham Railway, the company for which he was Locomotive Superintendent. Already an established engineer he had ten years of considerable autonomy in charge of the Great Western's Northern Division Works at Wolverhampton but worked closely with Gooch and seems to have been the obvious choice for CME, moving to Swindon on Gooch's resignation in 1864.

None of the other five CMEs had identical careers: Collett's progression was via the Drawing Office which he joined as a junior draughtsman at the age of 22 while Churchward's apprenticeship began at the age of 16 on the South Devon Railway, early training which

Above: *Gooch standard gauge Class 69 2-2-2 No 72 running with a cab around 1890*

impressed on him the importance of good adhesion and tractive effort on steeply graded routes. At the age of 19, in 1876, he transferred to the Swindon Drawing Office following the Great Western's takeover of the South Devon Railway.

Successful locomotive designs are inevitably credited to particular CMEs though in practice the best engine designs were usually the result of collaborative work by a team of supporting draughtsmen and mechanical engineers. This was generally the situation at the Great Western where progression to CME involved team work and often the role of Chief Assistant to the preceding CME. This was true for Collett who was Chief Assistant to Churchward who, in his turn, had been Chief Assistant to William Dean.

Equally, though, individual CMEs would often display outstanding individual flair and there is no doubt that George Jackson Churchward was the outstanding locomotive engineer of his era, introducing technical innovations adopted by other railways and establishing the appearance and characteristic of the Great Western's steam locomotives that would survive through to the end of steam in the 1960s.

So successful were Churchward's two and four cylinder express locomotives that a criticism of the Great Western's policy of internal succession was the inability of Churchward's successors, Collett and Hawksworth, to introduce truly innovative new designs. Collett's Castle and King classes, though enlarged and improved, were a logical development of Churchward's Star class locomotives while Hawksworth's County Class 4-6-

0 of 1946 was simply the final iteration of Churchward's two cylinder Saint class.

For the proper progressive development of Churcward's ideas and designs we need to turn to the work of another Great Western apprentice, Sir William Stanier. Born in Swindon and apprenticed to the Great Western at 16, Stanier was Swindon Works Manager for over 10 years before being poached by the London, Midland & Scottish Railway to become their new CME in 1931. Drawing on his Great Western experience of standardisation and engineering quality, Stanier revolutionised the motive power of the LMS, beset up to then with the "small engine" policy of the Midland Railway and lower engineering standards of the London & North Western Railway. And then he went on to produce the outstanding and most powerful Pacifics of the pre-war era, the Duchess class, arguably the true inheritors of Churchward's engineering vision.

Daniel Gooch's standard gauge locomotives

Though a strong advocate of the broad gauge, the Great Western's acquisition of the Shrewsbury & Chester and Shrewsbury and Birmingham railways in 1854 left Gooch the responsibility for providing new standard gauge engines. These new engines were built at either Swindon, Wolverhampton's enlarged Stafford Road Works or else commissioned from third party contractors.

Though notionally credited to Gooch most historians believe there was considerable collaboration between Gooch and Joseph Armstrong, the Locomotive Superintendent who came with the acquired standard gauge railways and certainly after 1858 all the locomotives produced at Wolverhampton would have been largely Armstrong's own work.

Apart from two 0-4-0 shunting saddle tanks built by Beyer Peacock all the other engines delivered between 1854 and 1864 were six wheelers, either 2-2-2 passenger engines of the "Jenny Lind" type, a few 2-4-0 mixed traffic engines while the greatest number were 0-6-0 goods and tank engines.

Among the first were eight 2-2-2 engines of the 69 class built by Beyer Peacock & Co during 1855-56. Originally intended for Wolverhampton to Shrewsbury passenger

services their route was extended

Above: *No 3373, Atbara, the first engine of the Atbara Class*

south from 1861 when they began running through to Paddington on the new mixed gauge track.

With new boilers and cabs fitted from 1880 onwards the class survived until the mid-1890s when they were rebuilt as 2-4-0s by William Dean.

By number the largest class of engines built during this period were 28 Gooch designed 0-6-0s of the 131 Class. Built between 1862 and 1865, 16 of the engines were built at Swindon while 12 were delivered from Slaughter, Gruning & Co in 1862. Instead of the usual Gooch valve gear these engines had Stephenson valve gear, indicating Armstrong's influence.

Joseph Armstrong's standard gauge locomotives

Un-championed because none of his locomotives have survived into preservation, Armstrong is sometimes unfairly regarded as an unexciting engineer. In fact he was an accomplished and experienced engineer who demonstrated considerable independence of thought, particularly after 1858 when he became fully responsible for the design and construction of standard gauge locomotives at Wolverhampton's Stafford Road Works.

After his premature death in 1877, at the age of 60, Armstrong was credited with leaving the Great Western well provided with locomotives appropriate for every purpose and service. These included over 300 of his 388 Class Standard Goods, generally regarded as the precursor for William Dean's more famous Standard Goods. Less well documented than other British locomotives that saw service overseas during the First World War, six were sent to Serbia while 16 were sent to Salonika. Stationed at Oxley, Stourbridge and Wellington, the final survivors of the class lasted until 1934.

Another Armstrong design that was produced in considerable volume were his Class 455 2-4-0 tanks, popularly known as "Metro Tanks" because they were originally introduced for London suburban working including running on the underground section of the Metropolitan Railway. 1869 saw production of the first batch of tanks and production at Swindon continued with modest batches of 20 through to 1899, well after Armstrong's death, because his successor, William Dean, regarded the tanks as such useful workhorses.

Originally built without cabs, Armstrong thought these had a bad effect on crew attentiveness, perhaps recalling his earlier career as an engine driver, later versions, used all over the Great Western network were built with both half and full cabs.

The class eventually totalled 140 engines and though withdrawals began as early as 1900, 10 locomotives from William Dean's last batch survived until 1948.

Other Armstrong designs were produced in small numbers, often for specific purposes or routes. These included the twenty 927 Class "Coal Goods" a variant of the Standard Goods with 4' 6" instead of 5' driving wheels specifically designed for hauling heavy trains of Welsh steam coal from Pontypool to the Mersey for transatlantic shipping and six mixed traffic 439 Class 2-4-0s built in 1868 for the route from Wolverhampton to Chester and known as the "Bicycle Class" because of the curious running plate curving over the 6'1" driving wheels.

Among the last engines designed by Armstrong and his last design of 2-2-2s for the Great Western were the ten engines of the Queen Class. Underlining the way in which locomotive designs evolve across eras rather than being specifically attributable to a particular CME these engines, which worked passenger expresses for over 30 years, can fairly be regarded as the precursors of Dean's 157 Class 2-2-2s.

William Dean's standard gauge locomotives

William Dean, a South London boy, was apprenticed to Joseph Armstrong at the Great Western's Wolverhampton Works. Clearly able, he was appointed as Joseph Armstrong's Chief Assistant at the age of just 23. When Gooch's sudden resignation saw Joseph

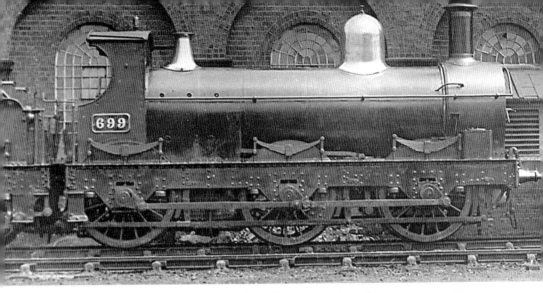

Armstrong promoted and relocated to Swindon, Dean was appointed Works Manager at Wolverhampton's Stafford Road Works where he worked closely with Joseph's brother, George Armstrong.

By 1868 Armstrong had re-secured Dean as his Chief Assistant at Swindon and they continued with the collaborative approach established at the beginning of the decade. During the 1860s and 1870s all the engines produced at Swindon and Wolverhampton as well as commissioned from outside suppliers were six wheelers: 2-2-2s, 0-6-0s and increasingly 2-4-0s, all comparable to similar engines used by other railway companies at that time.

In 1877 and as Chief Assistant, William Dean was thrust into the role of Chief Locomotive Superintendent following Armstrong's sudden death from a heart attack at 60. Dean's training and close association with Armstrong ensured that for the first few years his locomotive output closely followed the designs established by Armstrong. Locomotives such as the 157 Class 2-2-2s, a straight development of Armstrong's Queen Class and the 2201 Class 2-4-0s based on Armstrong's 806 Class but with an added cab and domeless boiler.

And now for two engines that have

Above: *Joseph Armstrong Class 388 Standard Goods No 699*

Above: *Bicycle Class 2-4-0 still running with raised running plate in 1890*

ensured that Dean's name is familiar with railway enthusiasts in a way that Armstrong's never has been. The workhorse 0-6-0 Dean Goods and the pretty and elegant looking 4-2-2 singles of the Achilles Class immortalised by Triang's Lord of the Isles locomotive and clerestory coach set introduced in the 1970s

First introduced in 1883 the Dean Goods broke with the Armstrong tradition in only having inside frames. Between 1883 and 1899 260 of the engines were built with progressive modifications and improvements to the boilers of each lot. The first 20 engines had domeless boilers

but eventually all engines were fitted with the class's archetypal large domed boiler.

Numbers of the engines were requisitioned by the Railway Operating Division (ROD) during the First World War and again by the War Department (WD) during the Second World War. At the end of the Second World War some engines remained abroad, in Austria, Silesia and even China.

Fifty four of the engines survived into BR ownership and were mainly used on lightly laid Welsh branch lines until replaced by Standard Class 2 2-60s. The last engine in service, no 2538, was withdrawn in May 1957. One engine has been preserved, no 2516, and can be seen as a static exhibit at the Swindon Steam Railway Museum.

Faster and prettier than a prosaic goods engine, the Achilles was Dean's other famous engine class. Development started with the production of 30 2-2-2 singles, Class 3001 in two separate batches in 1892 – 92. Though they represented the culmination of a Great Western tradition of 2-2-2s going back to *North Star* of 1837 they were also, in a sense, part of the renaissance of single wheelers on British Railways brought about by the invention of steam sanding in 1886.

Although the end of the broad gauge was in sight eight of the engines were built as broad gauge engines, ready to be converted to standard gauge following its final demise. Accommodating the demand for both broad gauge and standard gauge locomotives as economically as possible, including the design of "convertible" engines, was a significant compromise that Dean had to cope with during the 1870s and 80s.

With their long boiler the engines were top heavy at the front end and unstable at speed as demonstrated in September 1893 when No 3021, *Wigmore Castle,* was derailed in Box Tunnel. The

engine was rebuilt as a 4-2-2 with a front bogie in March 1894 and the rest of the class were similarly rebuilt during the rest of the year. These rebuilt engines provide the template for the 3031 Class, the first of which, *Achilles*, was built in March 1894. A total of 50 engines were built between 1894 and 1899 which when combined with the 30 Class 3001 engines reclassified as Class 3031 provided 80 elegant late Victorian engines designed to handle the Great Western's fastest expresses.

The single wheeler renaissance was short lived and the Achilles Class soon proved inadequate for the longer, heavier and more luxurious passenger trains running at the start of the twentieth century. Churchward made some preliminary but ultimately unsuccessful investigations to convert the class into 4-4-0s and all 80 engines were withdrawn and scrapped between 1908 and 1916. None were preserved though a static replica of No 3041, *The Queen*, was built in 1982 for installation at Tussaud's Railways and Royalty Exhibition at Windsor.

Although Gooch had built some broad gauge 4-4-0s the Great Western was late in employing the classic British inside cylinder 4-4-0. Dean's first foray was four engines classified as the Armstrong Class

and rebuilt in 1894 from individual Dean experimental engines, two of which, Nos 7 and 8, had been built in 1886 to test different steam compounding systems.

These four prototype engines were quickly followed by the Duke Class, 80 engines built in four batches of 20 between 1895 and 1899. With their outside frames and large domes the engines seemed to echo the archaic features of the last broad gauge locomotives and looked old-fashioned when compared to the contemporary designs of, for example, Matthew Holmes for the North British Railway and H A Ivatt for the Great Northern Railway.

Churchward was appointed Chief Assistant to Dean in 1897 and the next development of the Duke Class, the Bulldog Class, suggests his strong involvement. The first engine, *Bulldog,* was built in 1898 and a further 120 were added to the class between then and 1906, years that straddled the regimes of both Dean and Churchward. This was the period when Churchward was researching the improvement and standardisation of Swindon built boilers and with their mix of curved and straight frames, domed, domeless, parallel and tapered boilers it can be difficult classifying the Bulldogs. To add to the confusion, 20 Duke Class locomotives were rebuilt with Belpaire fireboxes and domeless tapered boilers between 1906 and 1909 and then reclassified as Bulldogs, bringing the total class to 141 engines.

Further variants of the 4-4-0 type were launched during Dean's final years as CME: twenty engines of the Badminton Class built between 1898 and 1899 and thirty engines of the Atbara Class built from 1900 onwards. When built the Atbara's had straight frames, Belpaire fireboxes and parallel domeless boilers and in appearance anticipated Churchward's famous City Class of 4-4-0s, including No 3440, the record breaking *City of Truro.*

George Jackson Churchward CBE (1857 – 1933)

George Jackson Churchward was born in Stoke Gabriel, on the River Dart, Devon, in 1857. His father was the local squire and there was no history of engineering in the family but as a boy Churchward showed an interest in mechanical devices and making things as well as enjoying countryside pursuits such as shooting and fishing.

He was educated at Totnes Grammar School, where he excelled at maths, joining the South Devon Railway as an apprentice at its Newton Abbott Works when he left school at the age of 16.

Three years later, in 1876, the South Devon Railway was acquired by the Great Western and Churchward moved to Swindon to complete his apprenticeship and transferred to the Swindon Drawing Office in 1877. By 1882 he had become Inspecting Engineer for materials but later that year was promoted to Assistant Carriage Works Manager, progressing to Carriage Works Manager in 1885 when James Holden left to join the Great Eastern Railway.

By 1895 Churchward moved to the locomotive works as Assistant Works Manager but quickly became the Locomotive Works Manager following the retirement of James Carlton as Works Manager in the same year. Though never formally described as such Churchward had become William Dean's principal assistant by 1897.

Historians have long debated to what extent William Dean's final designs, particularly the 4-4-0s, were primarily the work of G J Churchward. Dean was apparently generous in both encouraging and giving credit to his subordinates and it is probable that from 1895 to 1900 Dean and Churchward worked closely in a collaborative way much as Dean had worked with Joseph Armstrong in the 1870s. From 1900 until his retirement in 1902 Dean was heavily involved in the design and commissioning of the new, huge Shop A and during that period Churchward probably did assume full responsibility for the locomotive fleet as is evidenced by his large pay rise in 1900 and assurance that he get Dean's job when he retired.

In 1902 Churchward duly stepped into Dean's shoes, taking on the role of Locomotive, Carriage and Wagon Superintendent, a title altered to the

rather more succinct Chief Mechanical Engineer in 1916. Churchward retained the job until his own retirement just shy of 65 in 1921. And in those two decades Churchward revolutionised the production, management and maintenance of the Great Western locomotive fleet, establishing his reputation as one of Britain's most successful and competent railway engineers.

Churchward never married but like both Dean and Armstrong before him he took very seriously both his social responsibility and responsibility for Swindon Works. When the Swindon Railway Village, called New Swindon was combined with the original Swindon in 1900 Churchward became the first mayor of the new borough.

Left: *Official Works photo of Pacific No 111, The Great Bear*

During the First World War Swindon Works was heavily involved in manufacture for the war effort, a contribution that was marked by the award of CBEs to Churchward and three of his senior managers, including Charles Collett who was to succeed Churchward as CME.

After retirement Churchward continued living in the house originally provided by the Great Western for Joseph Armstrong, by the main line and close to the Works, which he continued to visit on a regular basis. On the 19th December 1933, while walking along the track to the Works he was knocked down and killed by a Paddington to Fishguard express. By now quite deaf and suffering from poor eyesight it is thought he never heard the train.

A radical new engine policy

By the time Churcward became Swindon Works Manager in 1895 he will have been familiar with the collection of oddities that made up the Great Western's locomotive stock: myriad classes of locomotives, some with no more than six or eight locomotives together with odd hybrids built as standard gauge engines, converted to broad gauge and then back to standard gauge, sometimes with the wheel arrangement changed. Even the term standard was observed more in principal than practice: Dean's 80 singles of the Achilles Class boasted, for example, no fewer than 12 different designs of front bogie.

By 1895, too, it would have been clear to Churchward that he could expect to take over Dean's role following his retirement, giving him two decades to establish a sensible, structured engine strategy by the time of his own expected retirement in 1921 or 22. He took advantage of the seven years he was Works Manager, working in collaboration with Dean to undertake his experimental work and, particularly, his work on the standardisation of boilers. During those years he supervised the production of over 250 4-4-0s of four or five different classes, each with different but potentially interchangeable boilers.

Once Dean's post had been assured to him in 1900 he drew up his standardised locomotive policy. His engine classes would be restricted to less than a dozen, using standardised boilers, wheels, cylinders, motion and tenders. As subsequent history demonstrated Churchward's strength was making full use of the best contemporary engineering techniques. He was not an experimental or visionary engineer in the mould of Bullied or even Brunel with their occasional heroic failures, but relied for his key ideas on American influence for boiler design and the latest French developments regarding cylinders and valve configuration.

So well planned was Churchward's strategy that it was fully accomplished before the First World War and the Great Western equipped with a superlative range of locomotives for express passenger, mixed traffic and freight duties. And so well-conceived were the designs that with just minor developments and improvements they lasted through to nationalisation in 1948 and beyond. Collett's Castle Class, for example, a development of Churchward's four cylinder Stars introduced in 1923, continued to be built right through to 1950. Inevitably this has led to criticism that Churchward's two successors, Collett and Hawksworth, failed to properly develop his original concepts. Looking at Hawksworth's County Class, little more than an updated development of Churchward's 2 cylinder Saints it has to be admitted there is something in the criticism.

For the imaginative development of Churchward's legacy we have to look at the work of Sir William Stanier on the LMS, which he joined in 1931 after ten years as Swindon Works Manager.

Churchward's locomotives

From his appointment in 1902 Churchward began working on prototypes for his standard designs. Typically just one, two or maybe three prototypes would be built and extensively tested and modified before volume production of the class. 1902-03 saw, for example, three prototype 2 cylinder 4-6-0s and a single prototype for a class of 2-8-0 heavy freight locomotives.

The first Churchward class delivered

in any volume were twenty 4-4-0 engines of the City Class produced in 1903 though even here testing was undertaken in 1902 when one of Dean's Atbara 4-4-0s, No 3405, Mauritius, was reboilered with a tapered boiler and a Belpaire firebox. This was the first 4-4-0 to be fitted with a tapered boiler which after some modification became the Swindon Standard Number 4 boiler fitted to the City Class.

The City Class included No 3440, City of Truro, famous as the first locomotive to allegedly achieve a speed in excess of 100mph. This was a planned speed run, hauling a lightly loaded "Ocean Mails" from Plymouth to Paddington on the 9th May 1904. A speed of 102.3 mph was briefly recorded by the notable railway commentator Charles Rous-Marten who had been specially invited to join the train by the Great Western

But for this event, which ensured the preservation of *City of Truro*, the engine would have been scrapped along with its fellow Cities in the 1930s and the class largely forgotten today.

Churchward's first 1902 4-6-0 prototype was No.100, *Saint Martin*, which provided the name Saints for subsequent engines of the class. *Saint Martin* had a domeless parallel boiler and piston valves while the subsequent two prototypes were fitted with half-cone boilers and redesigned valve gear layout and cylinders where the valve diameters were increased from 6½" to 10". The third prototype, No 171, was soon rebuilt as a 4-4-2 and had its boiler pressure increased from 200psi to 225psi to enable comparative tests with the De Glehn compound Atlantic that Churchward had persuaded the Great Western to buy from their French manufacturer. While the comparative compound v simple tests were underway an order for 19 similar engines was placed, 13 built as 4-6-0s and 6 as 4-4-2 Atlantics. Churchward preferred the additional adhesion offered by six-coupled engines and all the Saint Atlantics were subsequently rebuilt as 4-6-0s.

The "Saints", eventually numbering 76, engines were a successful class, providing the template for the later Hall Class and Hawksworh's County Class. Though withdrawals started in the 1930s a number survived into British Railways days with No 2920, Saint David, being the last engine withdrawn in October 1953. No Saints have survived into preservation but the Great Western Society at Didcot

Left: *City of Truro
No 3440 steaming
in preservation*

is currently converting a surviving Hall Class locomotive, No 4942 *Maindy Hall*, into a Saint, No 2999, *Lady of Legend*.

At some point during the nineteenth century freight had overtaken passengers as the Great Western's largest source of revenue and there was a constant clamour for freight engines, particularly for handling the heavy South Wales coal trains. Churchward envisaged a 2-8-0 for heavy freight and the 1902 prototype, No 97, was Britain's first 2-8-0 and underwent extensive testing before production of the first batch of the 2800 Class began in 1905. Totalling 84 engines the 2800s remained the Great Western's principal heavy freight locomotives through to the 1930s and the introduction of Collett's 2884 Class.

1904 saw the introduction of another of the dozen or so classes envisaged by Churchward, the 2-6-2 tank designed for branch line work. These first 11 engines, known as "Small Prairies" were specially designed for hilly lines such as the Princeton and Much Wenlock branches with their small 4'8½" driving wheels. These were followed by the larger and more numerous "Large Prairies", 75 of them built in five batches between 1906 and 1924. Characteristic of Great Western branch line workings the Large Prairies have been long time favourites with Great Western railway modellers.

Following extensive testing of the De Glehn Atlantic and the Atlantic versions of the Saint Class Churchill concluded that simple steam expansion, working with a balanced, four cylinder layout, would be simpler and more effective than

Above: *Charles Collett*

of the Stars continued until 1923 by which time the class totalled 72 engines. Developments of the Star Class by Churchward's successor, Charles Collett, lead to the development of the famous Castle and King Class locomotives.

A one-off little remembered today is the Great Western's single Pacific, no 111, *The Great Bear*, built in 1908, almost a decade and a half ahead of Sir Nigel Gresley's first Pacific for the North Eastern Railway. *The Great Bear* was built for publicity reasons to satisfy the Great Western's demands to have the largest and most powerful locomotive in Britain. With his dislike of trailing wheels and non-standard engines Churchward probably felt, at best, ambivalent about the engine though it is reported that he was saddened by its conversion to a 4-6-0 Castle Class in 1924 because of its very limited route availability.

When Churchward became the Locomotive, Carriage and Wagon Superintendent in 1902 he fully understood the advantages of reducing the locomotive stock to the smallest possible number of classes and of making components interchangeable between different classes so great that such standardisation would be the

compound steam. His first prototype No 40, prophetically called "North Star" because it would be just as significant to the Great Western as the Stephenson's *North Star* of 1837, was built as a 4-4-2 to maintain a continued fair comparison of the De Glehn engine.

No 40 established the benefits of four cylinders and from 1907 production of the Star class got underway, but as 4-6-0s instead of Atlantics, with No 40, *North Star*, being rebuilt as a 4-6-0 in 1909.

Very successful as the Great Western's top link passenger engines, construction

HISTORY OF THE **GREAT WESTERN RAILWAY**

defining characteristic of his engineering stewardship. He realised, too, that it could take 15 or 20 years to fully replace the existing stock of 3,000 or so engines so that his new designs would also need to be fit for purpose in twenty or thirty years' time, beyond his retirement.

He needn't have worried. In the event his designs provided a solid engineering template that would last the Great Western for half a century.

Charles Collett (1871 – 1952)

Charles Collett was born near Paddington but like his predecessor Churchward, did not come from an engineering or railway family and was, instead, the son of a journalist. He received a good education, attending Merchant Taylors School and then studying at London University before starting as a pupil at the works of Maudsley, Sons and Field, well known marine engine builders based at Lambeth.

In 1893, at the age of 22, Collett moved to the Great Western, joining the Swindon Drawing Office as a junior draughtsman. After four years and clearly competent he was given charge of the section responsible for buildings followed just a year later with promotion to the position of Assistant to the Chief Draughtsmen. By now he would have been well known to Churchward and in June 1900 he was made Technical Inspector at the Locomotive Works and then within a few month quickly progressing to Assistant Manager. He stayed in this role for 12 years before becoming Works Manager, a role he kept for 7 years. During those two decades, while working closely and collaborating with Churchward he developed an approach to the manufacturing side which would be crucial to the Great Western in the inter war years.

Appointment in 1919 to the post of Deputy Chief Mechanical Engineer would have confirmed his succession to the role of CME following Churchward's resignation.

When Collett assumed the role in 1922 he benefited from Churchward's legacy of a range of successful engine classes. Collett developed and improved those prototypes but was also able to devote attention to improving the quality and cost of Swindon's engineering processes. Relying on the Churchward bequest meant he also had time to absorb and standardise the thousand or so disparate locomotive types inherited from a range of smaller, mainly Welsh, railway companies following the Railway Grouping of 1922 – 23.

The General Strike of 1926 followed by the Depression created considerable financial pressure on the Great Western but the twenty year "apprenticeship" Collett spent at the Works ensured that he could manage the available resources very thriftily and make sure the company was never wanting for motive power.

Collett retired as CME in 1941, at the age of 70 after almost 20 years in the job. Though sometimes criticised for not maintaining the pace of development established by Churchward it would be fair to say that once again Swindon Works had produced an engineer of exceptional ability.

Collett's locomotives

Collett's first task was to design a new express passenger 4-6-0 with a maximum axle load of 20 tons to ensure the widest possible route availability. Starting with the reliable four cylinder Stars Collett enlarged them by increasing the cylinder bore to 15" and adding 12%

to the grate area. Enlargement of the grate required a 12" extension to the frames which allowed the provision of a larger and more modern looking cab with side windows. The first engine of the class, No 4073, *Caerphilly Castle* left Swindon in May 1923 and having spent a number of years as a static exhibit at the Science Museum, South Kensington has now been moved to the Steam Museum at Swindon.

So good was the improvement from these apparently minor changes the Castles continued to be built with minimum modification for the next 27 years by which time the class totalled 171 engines.

Next the operating department demanded an even more powerful passenger express, this time with a maximum permitted axle load of 22½ tons following the upgrade of the remaining four bridges and Paddington to take this weight. Collett developed the Star and Castle class concept even further: the biggest boiler ever built by Swindon, piston dimensions increased to 16" by 28" and boiler pressure raised from 225 psi to 250 psi. These features produced an engine with a tractive effort of 39,700 lbs but at this point management stepped

in and demanded the engine should have a tractive effort in excess of 40,000 to substantiate the Publicity Department's claim that it would be Britain's most powerful locomotive. An increase in the cylinder diameter from 16" to 16¼ did the trick, producing a tractive effort of 40,300 lbs for the King Class locomotives. There is a strong suspicious the design of the Kings had more to do with promotion than operational logic. Collett was strongly wedded to the ethos of standardisation but the King Class had its own one off boiler its own leading bogie specially designed to accommodate the large diameter cyliders and was limited to the main line routes to Bristol and Plymouth. Underlining its slightly awkward status, production of the class, in contrast to the Castles was capped at just 30 engines.

King George V, the first of the class was delivered from Swindon in May 1927 and almost straightaway, in August 1927, was shipped to the United States to feature in the centenary celebrations of the Baltimore & Ohio Railroad. During these celebrations it was presented with a plaque and a bell which it carried throughout its working life and into preservation.

The King Class may have had limited route application but Collett's next locomotive to start leaving the works in volume from 1928 was the Hall Class, a classic mixed traffic engine with comprehensive route availability. Underlining the development of the Halls as a progression from Churchward's two cylinder Saints, the class prototype dated back to 1924 when No 2925, *Saint Martin*, was rebuilt with smaller 6' driving wheels, realigned cylinders and a modern "Castle" type cab. Other modifications, including a switch to outside steam pipes and alteration of the boiler pitch were carried out during the testing period.

Production of the Halls continued throughout the thirties and including the Modified Halls, introduced in 1941 by Collett's successor Hawksworth, there were finally 259 engines in the class, all of which passed to British Railways ownership.

Collett continued to draw from the Saint's well with two other 4-6-0 classes specially designed for lighter laid routes. The Grange Class, with a Swindon No 1 boiler and 5' 8" driving wheels was one of the standard types identified by Churchward at the beginning of the century though it took until 1936 for Collett to fill the gap remaining in the plan. The 80 engines in the class largely assumed the duties of scrapped and withdrawn 4300 Class Churchward 2-6-0 Moguls.

The second class were the Manors produced in 1938. These used a specially designed boiler, Standard type No 14, and had an axle loading of just over 17 tons.

Only 30 of the class were built, the first 20 utilising driving wheels, motion and tenders from withdrawn Moguls. Used in Cornwall and on the old Cambrian Railway's lines in Wales an order for a further 20 engines was cancelled because of the outbreak of the Second World War.

As many of the engines, all withdrawn between 1963 and 1965, ended up in Barry Scrapyard and because their light axle loading makes them popular with heritage railways a total of 9 Manors have survived into preservation.

Frederick Hawksworth (1884 – 1976)

Unlike his five predecessors Hawksworth, the Great Western's sixth CME, was the only one to have been born in Swindon. And unlike Collett and Churchward he came from a family steeped in railways. His father was a Swindon Works draughtsman and his grandfather had been a Great Western foreman at Shrewsbury so it was more or less inevitable that Hawksworth would begin an apprenticeship at Swindon.

He started working in the testing house in 1898 but followed in his father's

footsteps and joined the Drawing Office in 1905. This was a good time for a young draughtsman to be in the Drawing Office as Churchward visited on an almost daily basis and was clearly impressed by Hawksworth and entrusted him with some of the working drawings for the *Great Bear* Pacific.

Beyond that progress was slow and steady and it was another 18 years before he got the post of Assistant Chief Draughtsman though by 1925 he was the Chief Draughtsman. As Chief Draughtsman Hawksworth worked closely with the Works Manager, William Stanier, and when he left to join the LMS in 1932 Hawksworth assumed the role of Collett's assistant.

As Collett's assistant and in the normal Swindon way Hawksworth would proceed to the role of CME but Collett hung onto the post until he was 70, in 1941, so Hawksworth was already 57 before he was appointed to the post.

Frustrated by the delay in his appointment he was then frustrated by being appointed in 1941, right in the middle of the Second World War with its shortage of materials and resources.. The limitation on the type of engines that could be sanctioned for construction during the War meant that , crucially, Hawksworth was denied his ambition of designing and building a Great Western Pacific, something to match the machines of Sir William Stanier and Sir Nigel Gresley.

Like Churchward, Hawksworth never married but committed himself wholeheartedly into both his career at the Great Western and his social responsibilities

Above: *No 6000, King George V, doyenne of the Class on static display at the Steam Museum, Swindon*

Hawksworth's locomotives

As Hawksworth's relatively brief tenure included the War years and a post-war period of limited resources his number of new designs for the Great Western were relatively few though do give some indication of what he might have achieved with more time and better circumstances.

Hawksworth met the demand for extra mixed traffic with an intelligent development of Collett's Hall Class. Dictated by wartime economies, construction of these engines, referred to as the "Modified Halls" made much greater use of fabrication instead of traditional castings. Construction of the class continued through the British Railways period up to 1950 when the class totalled 71 engines.

The one class of mainline passenger engines introduced by Hawksworth, the County Class, were used by Hawksworth as a test bed for features he wanted to include in his planned Pacific class.

Built to provide more powerful alternatives to the Halls and Granges the running gear of the Counties was almost identical to the Modified Halls

towards Swindon, including his teaching of design and machine drawings at the Swindon Technical Institute.

Hawksworth continued as CME after nationalisation and through the formation of the Western Region. As the new British Railways Board seemed to be recruiting the majority of its senior engineers from the former LMS and looking as though Hawksworth's position would soon vanish he chose to retire in late 1949, settling into a long retirement until his death in 1976 at the age of 88.

but the boiler was a development of the LMS Stanier Class 8F 2-8-0 boiler which Hawksworth had been able to study closely when the 8Fs were being built at Swindon as part of the war effort.

None of the 30 Counties built between 1945 and 1947 have survived but rather like the Tornado project the Great Western Society is recreating a new engine, No 1014, *County of Glamorgan*, from the frames of a Hall and the boiler of a Stanier 8F.

Hawksworth's other designs included three classes of pannier tanks, two of which were built after 1949 by the Western Region rather than the Great Western. The first design was the 9400 class of 1947, 10 of which were built by

the Great Western while the remaining 200 were built by British Railways. With their tapered domeless boilers they looked quite different to the traditional pannier tank though the heavier boiler came with a weight penalty that restricted their route availability. The 70 engines of the next class, the 1600, were a continuation of a design with a 70 year heritage going back to Joseph Armstrong and were available for use anywhere on the network. Hawksworth's final pannier tank design was for 10 engines of the 1500 class. Similar in appearance to the 9400 class these engines were designed with a short wheelbase for sharp curves and, uniquely for the Great Western, outside Walschaerts valve gear.

Traffic and Revenue

Construction of the Liverpool & Manchester Railway was primarily intended to break the freight rate stranglehold enjoyed by canal owners and provide cheap transport of raw materials and finished goods. It was always intended to carry passengers too, but the promoters were surprised by the unexpected demand though much of the early clamour was driven by the sheer novelty of travelling at speed by train.

Brunel, eager to enjoy the experience, was an early passenger on the London & Manchester and his belief that he could provide better passenger comfort and speed fired his vision for the broad gauge line from London to Bristol.

From its opening, freight traffic was important to the Great Western but Brunel's early judgement about meeting passenger demands was correct and it was not until 1912 that annual freight receipts of £7.4m finally overtook passenger receipts of £7m. By the 1930's, and in spite of increasing competition from road traffic, freight receipts accounted for 58% of the Great Western's revenue.

Passenger comfort

The superior quality and stability of broad gauge track offered passengers on the Great Western, third class excepted, a faster and more comfortable ride than on Britain's other early railways. Soon, though, improvements to standard gauge track and locomotive engineering meant that the Great Western's early advantage was quickly eroded and in the broad gauge's terminal years travel in aging and un-renewed stock provided a poor comparison with

Above: *Dean 3rd class coach of 1901 with traditional clerestory roof*

travel on conventional standard gauge railways, including the Great Western's.

From the 1860s the Great Western was increasingly involved in providing standard gauge travel and their stock was no better or worse than that on other standard gauge lines. During this era, when the Great Western's finances remained perilous, there was little incentive to replace aging broad gauge stock and little innovation in the construction of mainly four wheel standard gauge carriages. There was reluctance, too, to woo the increasingly important third class passengers, records in the early 1860s showing that the Great Western had only 200 third class carriages compared to 380 second class and 270 first class carriages. It was clear that middle and upper classes were the main source of the Great Western's passenger traffic but it met the working class traffic of the 1870s by cascading old second class carriages to third class use.

1874 saw a revolution in British carriage design when the Midland Railway imported Pullman cars fitted with pivoted four-wheel bogies that

HISTORY OF THE **GREAT WESTERN RAILWAY** 103

allowed carriages to take curves more easily and smoothly. The Midland and other railway companies quickly adopted bogie carries for their express passenger services. But not the Great Western where it was not until the 1880s when standard gauge stock was routinely built with bogies.'

Trend setting again, the Midland Railway abolished second class travel in 1875, a logical decision following the improvement in third class carriages and a consequent decline in second class passengers. From 1859 to 1874 the proportion of passengers travelling second class on Britain's railways fell from 32% to just 15% while over the same period the proportion of third class passengers increased from 49% to 76%, becoming, increasingly, the railway companies' main source of passenger revenue.

Other companies initially objected to the Midland Railway's decision but after analysing their own revenue mix and recognising the operational benefits of only having two classes most railways had dropped second class by the 1880s, but not the Great Western, which clung to three classes right up to 1910 though the competition finally forced it to improve its third class facilities and at last provide some semblance of upholstery on its third class seats.

From 1885 G J Churchward was the Swindon Carriage Works Manager and in 1891 the Great Western's carriage development finally showed that spark of innovation that had characterised the early broad gauge years. This was the introduction of the first British side corridor train with flexible gangways between the coaches and placed, initially, on the standard gauge route from Paddington to Birkenhead via Birmingham.

At the start of the twentieth century and now established as the company's chief engineer Churchward took advantage of the old broad gauge clearances with a bold design for the largest coaches seen in Britain, 70 ft long and 9 ft 6" wide. Carried on two four-wheel bogies the most dramatic advance was in the internal layout and access to the coaches. The new vehicles had side corridors which changed sides halfway along the coach with entry from the platform by end and centre door with access to the individual compartments only from the corridor.

The traditional clerestory roof, familiar on the Great Western for over 30 years, was replaced by a high elliptical profile, giving a more spacious interior and adding to the sense of size which earned the coaches the nickname "Dreadnaughts" after Britain's latest battleships.

Although the design anticipated the style of coaches familiar today the Dreadnoughts were not popular with the travelling public who did not like the end door entrances and preferred individual doors to each compartment.

No more Dreadnaughts were built and Churchward's "toplight "stock of 1907 established a style of corridor coaches with doors to each compartment that would persist until the end of the Great Western's independent existence in 1948. The "toplight" description related to the small toplight windows above the main window and though this feature was only standard for around 15 years it became virtually a Great Western trade mark because many of the coaches survived until the late 1950s.

Other technical improvements characterised by the start of the new century were the gradual introduction of electric lighting and the universal adoption of steam heating, ending the use of that classic feature of Victorian rail travel, the foot warmer, a sort of tin hot water bottle. Steel underframes replaced timber and by Collett's time in the 1920s steel panelling replaced wooden panelling on coach bodies although coach liveries retained panels picked out in contrasting lining as though the wooden mouldings were still there.

Coaches built in the 1920s varied in size from batch to batch, both in length, between 57 ft and 70 ft, and width from 9ft to 9ft 7in, the widest being primarily for former broad gauge routes with generous clearances such as the prestige Cornish Riviera service to the West Country.

Collett's final development of steel panelled coaches and one again taking full advantage of broad gauge clearances were the 8 open "Ocean Saloons" of 1931 designed for boat train traffic between Plymouth and London. Similar in design and profile, 61 ft 4½ in long and 9ft 7in wide, were the Centenary coaches celebrating the Great Western's hundredth anniversary and introduced on the Cornish Riviera Express from 1936.

In the early 1900s and in common with other railway companies the Great Western sought ways of countering road competition and reducing costs of suburban and branch line operation. Like those other companies the Great Western introduced steam railmotors, coach and steam power unit combined in a single coach. Between 1903 and 1908 the Great Western built 99 steam railmotors which were mainly deployed in rural areas and around Plymouth but underpowered on hilly routes and problems keeping the coach interiors clean saw most converted into driving trailers on pull-and-push sets with a separate locomotive.

Accidents of history saw one of the last steam railmotors to be built, No 93, survive as a "Work Study Coach" and latterly as a static office until sold to the Great Western Society in 1970 who between 1998 and 2011 were able to recreate a working steam railmotor.

The steam railmotors may have suffered from power problems but the provided a successful template for the introduction of diesel powered railcars in the 1930s. The prototype, No 1, inspired by Germany's streamlined "Flying Hamburger" and built by the Associated Equipment Co. Ltd (AEC) entered service in 1933. With minor modifications No 1 proved a success and was quickly followed by numbers 2,3 and 4, spearheading volume production

Left: *Preserved diesel railcar No 4 at the Steam Museum, Swindon*

from 1938 onwards using bodies built at Swindon and power units supplied by AEC.

Known affectionately as "Flying Bananas" with their predominantly cream livery the railcars remained in regular use until the 1960s when they were replaced by British Railway's first generation of diesel multiple units.

The freight scene

Bristol's commercial interests were tightly controlled by the Merchant Venturers, a guild dating back to the 15th century and granted a royal charter as "The Merchant Venturers' Society of Bristol" by Edward VI in 1552. By the middle of the 18th century Bristol had established itself as the second city to London and the leading British port for the Atlantic slave trade. But from the 1730s Bristol began to lose influence to Liverpool with its more easily accessible deep water docks, lower port fees and less hidebound merchant traders. The Merchant Venturers hoped to reverse the damage and restore Bristol's position

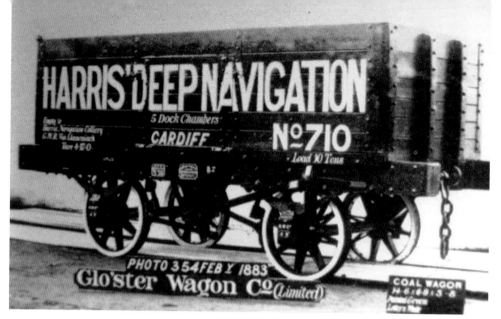

HARRIS'DEEP NAVIGATION
5 Dock Chambers
CARDIFF   No 710
Load 10 Tons

PHOTO 354 FEB Y 1883
Glo'ster Wagon Co (Limited)

COAL WAGON

Above: PO wagon of the South Wales Deep Navigation mine dating from 1883

as Britain's second port by building a railway from Bristol to London.

Important though the railway was it came too late to re-establish Bristol's status and even Brunel's vision of a direct service from London to New York via Bristol was destroyed when the Cunard Line, based in Liverpool, won the cross Atlantic mail contract and established a reliable shuttle service across the ocean. Without the assured volume of port traffic the Great Western was heavily dependent on passenger revenue in the early years, perhaps correctly anticipated by Brunel

with his emphasis on passenger comfort.

In time, though, as the network extended and tapped into the coalfields of South Wales, factories of the West Midlands and agricultural produce from the West Country freight began to assume more and more importance so that by the end of the second world war heavy freight and mixed traffic engines outnumbered purely express passenger engines by more than three to one.

Families living close to goods yards were very aware that the bulk of freight traffic went by night. The Great Western was an early adopter of vacuum-braked freight stock and every evening starting at 8:05pm no fewer than 12 express goods trains left Paddington Goods Station over the next five hours destined for Birkenhead, Carmathen Junction, Plymouth, Cardiff, Weymouth, Wolverhampton, Newton Abbott, Worcester, Fishguard with three separate trains heading for Bristol.

With comparable timings a similar procession of trains would be setting out from Birkenhead, Bristol, Cardiff, Westbury, and Wolverhampton.

Dating back to the broad gauge, Great Western men had been adept at ascribing nicknames to the timed freight trains, such as the "The Flying Pig" for the 10:45pm Exeter Goods and the "Didcot Fly" for the nightly service from Paddington to Didcot.

In an attempt to arrest declining freight traffic during the 1930s the Great Western capitalised on these nicknames in a promotional booklet, "Guide to Economical Transport". This provided details of no fewer than 73 express vacuum fitted and accelerated freight trains, including all the popular nicknames used by Great Western staff and encouraged traders to consign goods on "The Spud", Cardiff to Chester, "The Carpet", Kidderminster to Paddington" or "The Moonraker", Westbury to Wolverhampton.

Many of these night freights were long non-stop runs typically hauled by Churchward's heavy freight 2-8-0 locomotives to cope with loads of up to 800 tons. Often used for summer holiday passenger traffic the 2-8-0s could travel at speed and comfortably managed the freight train speed limit of 60mph. Freight stock, vans and wagons designed for specific purposes, had to be maintained in first class condition to cope with regular fast speeds. The telegraphic code name for the different types of stock provides a fascinating study in itself: Mogo, a 12 ton motorcar van, Vent-Insulmeat, Asmo and Bloater for long wheelbase fish vans.

Coal traffic from South Wales had been important since the 1850s but suffered a serious revenue setback during the long coal strike of 1926. In the 19th century specially designed 0-6-0s were used but following their introduction the heavy 2-8-0s were exclusively allocated to this traffic. The 2-8-0s could manage heavy loads but required assistance to manage the heavy gradients on each side of the V profiled Severn Tunnel. A large stud of tender and tank engines were based

at Severn Tunnel Junction specifically for this purpose with coal trains stopping for the assisting engine, typically a Large Prairie, to be attached.

Up to the 1920s coal was universally carried in open four-wheeled 10 or 12 ton capacity trucks owned almost entirely by either the collieries or large coal merchants, the so-called private owner (PO) wagons. Coal wagons could not generally be used for any reciprocal traffic so the business involved returning and correctly distributing long trains of empties. The Great Western's forward thinking General Manager Sir Felix Pole, newly appointed in 1921, reasoned

that larger coal wagons, 20 or even 30 tons would take up less space on sidings and reduce the number of wagons to be moved, with potential time and cost savings of up to 35%. To encourage their adoption by the mines and merchants Sir Felix offered a 5% carrying charge reduction for coal conveyed in 20 ton wagons. So confident was Sir Felix of the scheme's adoption that in 1924 the Great Western ordered 1,000 20 ton wagons but initial responses from the mine owners was lukewarm and the plan foundered when the 1926 coal strike brought many South Wales mines to the brink of ruin.

Milk was another important year-

round freight with the Great Western daily delivering 240,000 gallons to London, far more than any other single transporter, rail or otherwise. Milk was traditionally delivered in milk churns carried in long wheelbase slatted or ventilated vans described as Siphons but from the 1930's these were replaced by six-wheel 3,000 gallon glass lined tanks capable of running at passenger train speeds. The county of Carmarthen was a big supplier of milk and each day the 3:50pm milk special from Whitland to Paddington, up to 18 milk tank wagons, would regularly be hauled by a Castle class 4-6-0 locomotive.

As well as milk, seasonal traffic was also an important feature of traffic from the West Country, flowers in the Spring, fruit in the early summer and special trains organised to transport broccoli and cauliflowers from Cornwall.

As well as managing normal day-to-day freight the Great Western, like most other railway companies, was adept at managing special one-off trains such as moving a circus or relocating a complete farm, both livestock and machinery, from one part of the country to another.

The Railways Act and Grouping

The legacy of the 1840s Railway Mania and the deep depression of the 1870s meant that by the turn of the 20th century the finances of many of Britain's railways were in a parlous state. Over 100 companies, large and small, were often competing in parallel for the custom of passengers and traders in the same region. The parallel railways of the East Midlands, the long standing rivalry between the South Eastern and London, Brighton & South Coast railways together with the Great Western and the London & South Western railways' territorial battles are just a few examples of such local and often futile competition.

This un-ending battle for local custom came to an end with the outbreak of the First World War when all Britain's railway companies, including the Great Western, came under Government control. This direct state control lasted until 1921 by which time there was a general acceptance that a return to the pre-war competitive situation would not be compatible with the creation of a more efficient and integrated railway system. Following debate, which included the possibility of nationalisation, the Railways Act of 1921 grouped the 120 or so existing railway companies into four large geographically based entities: the Southern Railway, the London, Midland & Scottish Railway, the London & North Eastern Railway and the Great Western Railway.

The Great Western, uniquely, retained its name and brand image but was expanded by the acquisition of mainly Welsh railways and the tidying up absorption of small independent railways already operated by the Great Western. Grouping was an enormously complex

operation and though the statutory date for Grouping was the 1st January 1923 the Great Western anticipated this by acquiring the bulk of its expanded network during 1922.

A Welsh Dowry

Grouping added almost 1,000 miles to the Great Western's existing track of 3,000 miles, the bulk of this coming from a number of railways serving the coal mines of South Wales and the Cambrian Railway with its network covering the Welsh coast and Mid Wales.

The three largest South Wales railways absorbed, the Taff Vale Railway (125 miles), the Rhymney Railway (51 miles) and the Barry Railway (68 miles) had been almost exclusively developed for the transport of coal and iron from the heads of the South Wales valleys to the Docks at Cardiff and Barry. Three other South Wales companies, the Cardiff Railway, The Alexandra Docks & Railway and the Rhondda & Swansea Bay Railway, came with less track mileage but had developed intensive networks round the industrial and dock complexes of Cardiff, Swansea and Port Talbot

With a history dating back to 1864 the 230 miles of the Cambrian Railway resulted from the progressive amalgamation of over a dozen smaller and

often impecunious railways, including the narrow gauge Vale of Rheidol and Welshpool and Llanfair railways. Serving a largely rural area, the Cambrian connected with both the Great Western and London & North Western railways to provide connections to North Wales and North West of England.

Running trains on the steep gradients of the South Wales valleys required engines with high adhesive weight, plenty of and good braking ability. All of the South Wales' companies found that small wheeled 0-6-2 tank engines, running happily in either direction, best met these demands. After grouping most of these engines were standardised, looking just like Great Western engines with their standard tapered Swindon boilers but as homage to their

effectiveness Collett introduced a Great Western version of the 0-6-2 tanks specifically for service in South Wales in 1933.

Narrow gauge and light railways

Each of the narrow gauge railways, the Vale of Rheidol and Welshpool and Llanfair , that came with the Great Western's acquisition of the Cambrian Railway have remained working today as part of Britain's extensive heritage railwaynetwork.

The 1ft 11¾ gauge Vale of Rheidol Railway was built to carry timber and ore from the Rheidol valley down to the sea but by the time in opened lead mining in the area was in steep decline. Fortunately this coincided with the introduction of annual holidays and Wales became a popular location, particularly for workers from the West Midlands, and established the railway as the tourist attraction it has been throughout its existence.

Unlike most other narrow gauge railways the Vale of Rheidol was included in the 1948 nationalisation and it remained in British Railways ownership until privatised in 1989. Its engines, uniquely, were the only British Railways steam engines to bear the post-1964 blue livery and double arrow icon.

Built under the 1896 Light Railways Act the 2ft 6" gauge Welshpool & Llanfair Light Railway was opened in 1903 to aid economic development in a remote farming area, never making a profit. Under Great Western ownership passenger services ceased in 1931 but freight services continued through nationalisation until finally withdrawn at the end of 1956.

By then both the Tallylyn and Festiniog had established the concept of railway preservation and in 1963 a group of volunteers reopened the western end of the line, from Llanfair Caereinion to Castle Caereinion as a tourist attraction.

Other small railways taken over at

Above: *Vale of Rheidol 2-6-2T locomotive sporting British Rail blue era livery*

Grouping included lines in England which, though independent, had been operated by the Great Western for a number of years. These included lines such as the Princetown Railway on Dartmoor, the Liskeard & Looe Railway and the Didcot, Newbury and Southampton Railway, routes which the travelling public probably imagined were already owned by the Great Western. Other fully independent railways acquired included the struggling Midland & South West Junction Railway and in Shropshire the quaintly named Cleobury, Mortimer and Ditton Priors Light Railway, another railway built under the 1896 Light Railways Act.

The Great Western Branch Line

The monthly magazine *The Great Western Journal*, with articles on historical and contemporary facets of the railway, confirms that the old company still has a more loyal following than, perhaps, other historical railway companies. And many older non-enthusiasts still have affectionate memories of the Great Western during the 1950s and early 60s when its engines, trains and operations seemed little changed from the pre-nationalisation era.

Why is there such a strong nostalgic feeling for the Great Western?

Perhaps it's the aesthetic beauty of the Churchward inspired express locomotives, hauling trains of familiar chocolate and cream coaches or maybe it's fond memories of summer holiday journeys from Paddington culminating in a leisurely journey along a bucolic branch line to such locations as Paignton, Kingsbridge, Falmouth, St Ives or Newquay.

Today the spirit of that warm, summer holiday feeling is splendidly evoked by the number of heritage railways operating Great Western locomotives and stock on former Great Western lines and adhering faithfully to Great Western working practices. The Dartmouth Steam Railway, South Devon Railway and West Somerset Railway are just three of the best examples.

The perfect attention to detail on these preserved lines reminds us, too, how popular the Great Western branch line has been with railway modellers, with their models, particularly, of country or seaside branch termini. And there were plenty of prototypes to provide modelling

Left: *Chudleigh Station on the Teign Valley branch captures perfectly the charm of the Great Western branch line*

inspiration, Ashburton, Yealmpton, Moretonhampstead, Hemyock, Newcastle Emlyn and Fairford. For modellers with limited space the appeal is very clear: the ability to accurately recreate a prototype with sharper curves than the mainline, smaller engines and shorter trains, just one or two carriages and that other favourite of railway modellers, the daily pick up goods.

But what were the other ingredients that provided the full size versions with the same magical appeal, other than just a leisurely ride through a sylvan setting on a beautiful summer's day? There were really two elements in the unique mix that made up the Great Western branch line: the track, station buildings and other artefacts constituting the physical railway and the traffic running along it.

Branch line infrastructure

Great Western branch lines were usually well engineered and built with the planned sparsity of level crossings not just related to the number of overbridges and viaducts in hilly country regions. Maintenance was kept to an exceptional level with well aligned and weed free track. Though later branches may have been commissioned after Brunel's death they were largely built by men with great respect for his standards of engineering. Structures may not have been quite to the same standard as the main Paddington to Bristol main line but were generally more robust than those on the branches of other railway companies.

Stations, goods and engine sheds

Right: *A model captures the magic of the Great Western branch line*

were substantial stone or brick buildings, carefully maintained structurally and kept scrupulously clean. Infrequent trains allowed time to create imposing station gardens and flower displays and even, occasionally well-tended vegetable patches on approaching embankments.

Signalling, too, was often more elaborate than on other railways with the distinctive lower quadrant semaphores instantly identifying a branch as Great Western. Generally station layouts were as neat and tidily arranged as a well-kept model railway, explaining the continuing appeal to modellers up to the present day.

Branch line traffic

Branch line infrastructure on the Great Western may have been a cut above average but the same claim could not be made for the trains running on them. Pulling one or two chocolate and cream coaches the small green-painted tank engines may have looked splendid with their copper capped chimneys and brass safety valves but it was the pace that left much to be desired, particularly if you were a passenger in a hurry. Taking on water and waiting for single-line tokens could add time to every journey so that average speeds rarely exceeded 20mph.

Such leisurely journeys meant there was little incentive to develop more powerful locomotives in sparsely inhabited areas and even the pannier tanks and 0-4-2 auto tanks constructed by Collett in the 1920s and 30s harked back to Joseph Armstrong's designs of the 1860s and 70s. These engines were, arguably underpowered and passengers became familiar with trains racing downhill and then crawling up even quite modest gradients. Legend confirms that on some lines the single unit steam railmotors had to stop on hills to give time for steam pressure to build up and then continue the journey.

Undemanding timetables meant, though, that everything ran like clockwork and that mainline trains were rarely delayed by the late arrival of a branch-line train. Running like clockwork meant that timetables were rarely tampered with, sometimes remaining unchanged for decades. Knowing the long-standing times and frequency of trains was a good way for country people to organise their lives with getting up, going to work, having meals and going to bed driven by the Great Western's timetable.

The timetable for each branch had its own pattern, a daily weekly and seasonal rhythm. Most branches had school traffic, workers and commuters and, at particular time of the year, the transport of perishables.

The pick up goods

From the earliest days of railways the pick up goods train was an enduring feature of branch line operation. The Great Western was no exception and most country stations had three or four sidings and goods shed for the delivery of coal and delivery and collection of goods and produce.

Usually daily, a locomotive would collect a rake of vans and wagons destined for stations and private sidings along the line, dropping them of and collecting wagons for the return journey as it passed through. Speeds were low and often the train would be held in the goods yard waiting for passenger trains to pass. This and seasonal peaks and troughs meant that the timetable for the daily pick up was understandably vague.

Most pick up goods included a single van with small consignments and parcels that could be dropped off at the platform without shunting the goods yard. The Great Western called this the Station Truck though on smaller branches the Brake van often undertook this duty.

Originally daily, competition from motor lorries in the 20th century saw the service reduced to two or three times a week to finally just weekly. Dr Beeching's 1963 Report, *The Reshaping of British Railways*, sounded the final death knell for the pick up goods with all local station goods yards closed and nationwide freight facilities reduced to just 100 locations designed to service only the new containerised Freightliner traffic.

Nationalisation and Beyond

The manifesto of the Labour Government returned to power in 1945's landslide victory included the nationalisation of Britain's principal's industries, coal, power, iron and steel and transport. Nationalisation of the railways was not a new idea, first mooted in the 19th century and seriously considered in 1921 before Grouping and the creation of the "Big Four" railway companies.

The Big Four, though actively opposed to rail nationalisation, were not unaware of the needs for more efficient integration of the rail network and, in anticipation of impending nationalisation, had undertaken their own study in 1942 to establish more efficient ways of co-operative working after the war.

In spite of fierce opposition from transport lobbies and the Conservative opposition The Transport Act 1947 was duly passed and the Big Four Railway companies were vested in the British Transport Commission (BTC). Under the Transport Act the BTC had the duty to provide an integrated system of transport in Britain which was to have due regard to safety and efficiency and to comply with a complicated instruction to "break even financially taking one year with another".

The BTC was organised into five separate functions: Railway Executive, Road Haulage Executive, Road Passenger Executive, Docks and Inland Waterways Executive and a London Transport Executive. Each Executive had considerable autonomy and as they tended to operate independently of each other the laudable aim of transport integration was quickly compromised.

Following privatisation in 1992

management of Britain's railways continues to arouse fierce debate with attitudes to nationalisation, almost 70 years later, remaining partisan.

The Railway Regions

After nationalisation the Big Four were split into six separate regions, Western, Southern, London Midland, Eastern, North Eastern and Scottish. Though British Railways quickly established distinctive overall branding, each region continued to retain the image and operational characteristics of its previous privately owned companies. Hardly surprising as the senior and middle managers had segued quietly from running the Big Four to managing the new Regions.

The Western Region

No company had been more resistant to the idea of nationalisation than the Great Western and in common with the other Big Four companies no director joined the BTC though one senior officer, David Blee, was appointed as Commercial Member of the Railway Executive.

Resolving four companies into six regions involved some geographical changes, increasing the Western Region's network from 4,000 to 4,350 miles and increasing the number of stations from 1,600 to over 1,900, making it the largest of the new regions. The main changes were the takeover, in 1948, of the London Midland's lines in Central and South Wales and in 1950 the London Midland's lines south-west of Birmingham and the Southern Region's lines west of Exeter.

The management of the Western Region had considerable autonomy and continued to run the Region in the "Western" way, demonstrating considerable independence, for example, on locomotive policy. While other Regions, during the Modernisation Plan's "dash for diesel", were developing diesel electric locomotives the Western Region remained stubbornly committed to diesel hydraulic engines such as the Warships, Westerns and Hymens. These non-

standard classes had short lives as they gave way to the more numerous, conventional and, arguably, more successful type 3 and 4 diesel electric locomotives.

The locomotives may have sported the cycling lion and stations adorned with sausage shaped name lozenges but 10 years after nationalisation the look and feel of the Western Region would, to the average passenger, felt little different to the old Great Western. It took the end of steam, Dr Beeching and completion of the modernisation plan to finally destroy that cosy familiarity.

Railway company First Group may have reprised the Great Western brand, cynically some might argue, but little of the old Great Western's characteristic magic has been retained. For that to be reprised the modern traveller needs to make a journey on one of the many heritage railways that have faithfully preserved the image of the Great Western and Western Region in its early days.

The Preservation Scene

Britain's nostalgic obsession for times past and an abiding passion for steam has seen the heritage railway movement grow to almost 200 separate sites since the 1950s. The first railway to establish the pattern of enthusiastic volunteers bringing history to life was the Tallylyn, a Welsh narrow gauge railway.

In spite of improvements' to holiday traffic the Tallylyn had limped through the 1930s and 40s, closing finally at the end of the summer in 1950. Rail enthusiast and author Tom Rolt quickly established The Tallylyn Railway Preservation Society and by May 1951 the Society, with 650 members, was able to reopen using volunteers to run the service. Preservation of the Tallylyn was quickly followed by the Ffestiniog Railway, another Welsh narrow gauge railway which had ceased operating in in 1946 but was reopened by volunteers in 1955.

The first standard gauge society was the Bluebell Preservation Society, set up in 1959 to preserve part of the East Grinstead to Lewes line which had been closed in 1958.

During the 1960s the Modernisation Plan and Dr Beeching's Report saw steam withdrawn from Britain's railways and branch line closures proceeding at a pace. This was accompanied by a rash of preservation societies set up to try and reclaim lines for future operation before British Railways could rip up the track. This included a number of societies dedicated to the preservation of former Great Western branch lines and facilities such as the closed locomotive shed at Didcot.

Great Western heritage sites

The first Great Western branch to be preserved was the Dart Valley Railway, the classic Great Western branch line following the River Dart through beautiful Devon scenery from Totnes to the terminus at Ashburton, beloved of railway modellers. The line had closed to all traffic in 1962 but was reopened by the Dart Valley Light Railway Company in April 1969 in a ceremony undertaken, ironically, by Dr Richard Beeching. The preserved railway accurately reflects the spirit of the Great Western and includes the operation of a typical motor train normally hauled by a preserved Collett 0-4-2 tank engine.

Starting at about the same time the next important heritage railway is the Severn Valley Railway. The Severn Valley, a single track railway, was built between Hartlebury, near Droitwich Spa, and Shrewsbury, a distance of about 40 miles. Progressive closure of the line started in 1962, prior to Dr Beeching's Report, and the Severn Valley Preservation Society was formed in 1965. Granted a Light Railway Order in 1969 the Society opened the section

from Bridgenorth to Hampton Loade. Since 1984 a regular service has been run between Bridgenorth and Kidderminster, a distance of around 16 miles.

The prize for the longest preserved Great Western Railway belongs to the West Somerset Railway which regularly runs trains from Bishops Lydeard to Minehead, a distance of 23 miles. Bishops Lydeard connects to the main rail network and occasional specials run the two or so miles from Bishops Lydeard to Taunton.

New Great Western heritage sites continued to open during the 1970s and

About: *Pannier Tank No 5786 awaiting to depart from Buckfastleigh to Totnes on the Dart Valley Railway*

80s so that there are now more than a dozen, including two in Wales, the Gwili Railway and picturesque Llangollen Railway.

Barry scrapyard

So prolific was the growth of these heritage railways that it seemed there would soon be a famine of preserved locomotives, especially Great Western

ones, to run on them. But in a curious quirk of history many of the steam engines withdrawn from the Southern and Western Regions ended up at the Woodham Bros scrapyard in Barry. Stripped of their valuable copper and brass fittings many mouldered there for over two decades while Dai Woodham got on with cutting up wagons and waited for the price of scrap to rise. Provided they could meet the prevailing scrap price enthusiasts could rescue their cherished locomotives from the scrapyard though subsequent restoration has often taken over 20 years.

Almost 100 Great Western engines have been rescued from Barry, including two Kings, five Castles, 15 heavy freight 2-8-0s, 17 Halls and no less than 23 Prairie Tanks. Not all of these engines are currently operational and some will only ever be retained as a source of spares.

Mainline running

Although British Rail was at first reluctant to allow the running of steam specials on mainline tracks they have now become a familiar feature of the heritage industry with several companies offering travel and dining opportunities throughout the year.

Most are hauled by express passenger engines, including Great Western Castles and Kings, some of them rescued from Barry. No 5029, *Nunney Castle*, rescued from Barry in 1976 is one such regular performer along with King class locomotives No 6023 *King Edward II* and No 6024 *King Edward I*, both of which were rescued from Barry.

The pictures in this book were provided courtesy of the following:

GETTY IMAGES
101 Bayham Street, London NW1 0AG

WIKICOMMONS
commons.wikimedia.org

THE GREAT WESTERN ARCHIVE
www.greatwestern.org.uk

Sandy J J Gould, Ballista, Mattbuck, Geof Sheppard, Derek Hawkins, Nancy, Turner Bequest 1856, Illustrted London, News (Topfoto), Chris J Dixon, Geof Sheppard, High Rse, Ben Brooksbank, Hugh Llewelyn, Chowells, W.M. Spriggs, Victor-ny, Antione, John Alsop Collection, Ashley Dace, Phil Scott, Tim Walker, www.warwickshirerailways.com/, Oxyman, David Merrett, Lester Brown, http://transport-of-delight.com/, Flying Stag, Lloyd Morgan, Tony Hisgett, Jonathon Simkins, Danny252, Floyd Nello, Les Chatfield.

Design & Artwork by Scott Giarnese

Published by Demand Media Limited

Publishers: Jason Fenwick & Jules Gammond

Written by Ian Mackenzie